A Primer
of Clinical
Interpretation

A Primer
of Clinical
Interpretation

Philip F.D. Rubovits-Seitz

JASON ARONSON INC.
Northvale, New Jersey
London

This book was set in 11 pt. New Baskerville by Alabama Book Composition of Deatsville, AL and printed and bound by Book-mart Press, Inc. of North Bergen, NJ.

Copyright © 2002 by Jason Aronson Inc.

10 9 8 7 6 5 4 3 2 1

Library of Congress Cataloging-in-Publication Data

Rubovits-Seitz, Philip F. D., 1921–
    A primer of clinical interpretation / Philip F.D. Rubovits-Seitz.
       p. ; cm.
    Includes bibliographical references and index.
    ISBN 0–7657–0361–0
    1. Psychoanalytic interpretation. I. Title.
    [DNLM: 1. Psychoanalytic Interpretation. 2. Psychoanalytic Therapy—
methods. WM 460 R897p 2002]
    RC489.I57 R835 2002
    616.89'17—dc21

                              2002018295

Printed in the United States of America on acid-free paper. For information and catalog write to Jason Aronson Inc., 230 Livingston Street, Northvale, NJ 07647-1726, or visit our website: www.aronson.com

To future generations of
depth-psychological therapists

Contents

Preface

The purpose of this primer is to provide an introduction to clinical interpretation for students who are just beginning the study and practice of psychoanalysis or dynamic psychotherapy, and for more experienced clinicians who are interested in further study of clinical interpretation. The literature on clinical interpretation is surprisingly meager and does not convey the central role of interpretation in our clinical work. We have taken these methods largely for granted and have assumed that they are easier and more reliable than they actually are. A young colleague recently asked me, for example, "Why should we study interpretation? Isn't it something we do 'by the seat of our pants'?" To answer the young colleague's question, I briefly reviewed the history of clinical interpretation in the depth psychologies.

During the first half-century of psychoanalysis, Freud and his followers assumed that their methods of inferring latent meanings and determinants were scientifically sound. Freud (1905) confidently and repeatedly claimed that "it is easy to learn how to interpret dreams, to extract from the patient's associations his unconscious thoughts and memories, and to practise similar explanatory arts; for these, the patient will always provide the text." When analysts had difficulty agreeing on the interpretation of the same case material, Freud dismissed their disagreements with the ironic comment, *"Quot capita, tot sensa*—"as many heads, so many opinions." At the end of his career, however, Freud (1940) acknowledged that

> Our justification for making such inferences and interpola-
> tions and the degree of certainty attaching to them of course
> remain open to criticism in each individual instance; and it
> cannot be denied that it is often extremely difficult to arrive
> at a decision—a fact which finds expression in the lack of
> agreement among analysts.

Nevertheless, he continued to insist that psychoanalytic methods of confirming interpretations are "in every respect trustworthy" (Freud, 1937).

The uncertainties of clinical inference did not surface clearly until the 1950s, when Edward Glover (1952) and Thomas M. French (1955), working independently of each other and employing different methods of investigation, reported disturbing indications that clinical interpretation may not be as easy or as reliable as Freud claimed. French was dismayed to find that individual analysts react differently to the same clinical data, and Glover expressed alarm at the variability of conclusions based on interpretations. French referred to this as "the consensus problem"; Glover called it the "Achilles heel" of psychoanalysis.

The reports by Glover and French led a group of psychoanalysts in Chicago to undertake a systematic investigation of the consensus problem. Coordinated by the present writer (Seitz, 1966), the research team attempted to make blind interpretations of various amounts and kinds of the same clinical data. We worked together for over three years but were never able to achieve satisfactory consensus on the blind interpretation of the same case material. Since then, numerous other investigators have documented the consensus problem.

Considering the limited reliability of clinical interpretations, it seems very appropriate, even necessary, for students and clinicians to study the process and problems of interpretation as thoroughly as possible.

The principal precepts of clinical interpretation that I emphasize in this primer include:

1. Giving priority to methods of *understanding latent meanings and determinants*, rather than to the techniques of communicating interpretations to patients.
2. *Basing interpretations on clinical data* rather than on clinical theories so that interpretations are specific to the individual patient.
3. Clinical data consist of what the patient actually says and does during sessions and what the therapist observes introspectively in his or her responses to the patient; everything else is inferred.
4. There is no "Royal Road to the Unconscious," despite Freud's rhetorical statement to this effect. No particular type of clinical data is more useful for depth-psychological interpretation than any other; for example, dreams are only one among a wide variety of data that provide clues to latent meanings and determinants.
5. *Limiting the use of theory* in formulating interpretations to the basic general concepts (background assumptions) of psychoanalysis, in contrast to the use of specific clinical theories.
6. Clinical interpretation attempts to *understand both latent meanings and determinants*.
7. *The importance of imaginative conjecture* (inductive "leaps") in the construal (constructive) phase of the interpretive process—what Freud referred to as "hitting on a clever idea."

8. The hermeneutic concept of the *interdependent relations between "whole" and "part" meanings*: the whole is derived from and constituted by the parts, the parts being delineated and integrated by the whole.
9. *The fallibility of constructions*, which necessitates checking and justifying the correctness of interpretive hypotheses.
10. Facilitating the gradual development of *self-interpretive competence* in the patient.

This primer is divided into two parts: Part 1 deals with the classical (Freudian) approach to clinical interpretation. Part 2 includes some of the best-known postclassical approaches, presented in order of their increasingly divergent views from the classical approach—with the exception of the final chapter on Pluralistic Approaches, which combine the classical and postclassical approaches.

REFERENCES

French, T. (1955). The problem of consensus. Paper presented to the panel on "Validation of Psychoanalytic Techniques," rep. J. Marmor. *Journal of the American Psychoanalytic Association, 5*, 496–505.

Freud, S. (1905). Fragment of an analysis of a case of hysteria. *Standard edition* (Vol. 7, pp. 301–324). London: Hogarth, 1956, p. 116.

———. (1937). Constructions in analysis. *Standard edition* (Vol. 23, 255–270). London: Hogarth, 1964, p. 263.

———. (1940). An outline of psychoanalysis. *Standard edition* (Vol. 23, 141–208). London: Hogarth, 1964, p. 197.

Glover, E. (1952). Research methods in psychoanalysis. *International Journal of Psychoanalysis, 33*, 403–409.

Seitz, P. (1966). The consensus problem in psychoanalytic research. In L. Gottschalk & A. Auerbach (Eds.), *Methods of research in psychotherapy* (pp. 209–225). New York: Appleton–Century–Crofts.

Acknowledgments

I am grateful to Jason Aronson, M.D., for helpful suggestions regarding the format of this primer, and, as always, to Randi Rubovits-Seitz, M.D., for her steady encouragement and support. Thomas M. French, M.D., first simulated my interest in the process and problems of clinical interpretation—an interest that never dimmed once I began studying this subject.

I

The Classical
Approach to Clinical Interpretation

Chapter 1

What Is Clinical Interpretation?

Clinical interpretation is a complex process of inquiry into the inner mental life of patients suffering from certain forms of psychopathology. To make this definition clearer, it is necessary to focus on some of the terms included in it.

Question: What is meant by the term *process* in this connection?

Answer: Dictionaries define a process as a series of progressive and interdependent steps by which some end is attained. By that definition, clinical interpretation is a process, for even though depth-psychological understanding sometimes seems to occur as a sudden flash of insight, close study reveals that the intuition is a culmination of less noticeable preceding steps that led to understanding.

3

Question: What are the serial steps in the interpretive process?

Answer: The sequence of steps involved in the interpretive process includes:

1. Generating, collecting, and observing clinical data;
2. Scanning the data for clues to underlying latent meanings and determinants;
3. Cognitive processing and transformation of the clinical data and clues;
4. Construing (constructing) latent meanings and determinants (e.g., by inference from the clues);
5. Checking the correctness of the constructions;
6. Choosing between alternative interpretive hypotheses to determine the most plausible hypothesis;
7. Justifying the most plausible hypothesis;
8. When feasible and appropriate, communicating latent meanings and determinants to the patient;
9. Progressively modifying interpretations as the treatment progresses.

Question: What does the term *inquiry* mean in relation to clinical interpretation?

Answer: In this context the term *inquiry* implies investigation, not just asking questions. Clinicians tend to think of interpretation mainly in terms of therapeutic interventions, that is, as communications of depth-psychological information to patients, but the interpretive process is first and foremost an attempt to gain depth-psychological information and understanding. During therapy sessions, for example, the therapist's mind is engaged in a process of continual interpretive inquiry, attempting to recognize and understand clues to unconscious meanings and determinants (in both the patient and the therapist). The therapist's job is thus primarily to learn, not to teach. Communicating such information to patients is an important but only sporadic feature of the interpretive process, and it, too, is but a step in the process of interpretive inquiry because patients' responses to such communications provide valuable feedback that contributes to corrective modifications of interpretations.

Question: What is meant by the patient's "inner mental life"?

Answer: This term refers to the most important background assumption (or basic concept) on which clinical interpretations rest, namely, that of an unconscious mind. Many people associate the concept of an unconscious mind primarily or exclusively with Freud's theoretical system, but as Lancelot Whyte (1960, pp. vii–xi) has documented in his volume *The Unconscious Before Freud,* over fifty other philosophers and investigators contributed to the development of this concept in the two hundred years prior to Freud. Since about 1960, an increasing number of cognitive scientists also now agree that "the most interesting thought processes are unconscious" (Fodor, 1983).

Question: What is meant by *depth psychologies,* and how are they related to clinical interpretation?

Answer: What most characterizes the depth psychologies is their emphasis on the unconscious. Clinical interpretation is the stock-in-trade of the depth psychologies, which include psychoanalysis and the dynamic psychotherapies. All schools of psychotherapy that consider themselves "dynamic" in orientation (see below) agree that the core of psychoneurotic pathology involves a lack or avoidance of self-knowledge. They further hold that it is possible and useful for people to be in touch with their inner feelings and attitudes even though such self-knowledge may cause discomfort. As Spinoza put it: "There is no remedy which can be conceived more excellent for the emotions than true knowledge of them. Everyone has the power of understanding himself and his emotions, and consequently of suffering less from them." Kierkegaard wrote similarly: "He who has learned rightly to *be* anxious has learned the most important thing."

Question: What proportion of mental activity is unconscious?

Answer: To answer that question, depth psychologists sometimes use the analogy of an iceberg; that is, the mind is seven-eighths submerged. According to this analogy, consciousness is only the tip of the iceberg. Another analogy that is useful in grasping the concept of the unconscious is to compare it with an organ like the liver, which functions silently and continually without our having any awareness of its presence or activities. Similarly, unconscious mental processes go on all of the time without our realizing it. During the daytime, the unconscious mental activity is mainly in the form of inner fantasy images. Both unconscious fantasies and conscious fantasies (daydreams) can occur as thoughts, images, or both. Mental activity during sleep, of course, is mainly in the form of dreaming.

Question: What is meant by the preconscious?

Answer: Unlike unconscious mental processes, preconscious activities can be made conscious by focusing attention on them. Unconscious mental activities cannot be made conscious in that way, but require specialized methods such as inference to be surmised consciously.

Question: Are there any other differences between the unconscious, preconscious, and consciousness?

Answer: Unconscious mental processes differ from those of consciousness and the preconscious in a number of additional ways:

1. One difference concerns the speed of functioning: unconscious mental processes are much faster; for example, highly complex dreams can occur in a matter of seconds.
2. Another difference has to do with the use of images rather than words. Words are associated mainly with the preconscious. The extensive use of images in the unconscious is a factor that contributes to the speed of unconscious mental functioning, for multiple thoughts can be condensed in a single image. In addition, images lend themselves to rapid parallel processing. By contrast, the expression of meaning in words requires relatively slow linear processing.
3. Still another difference is that mental associations in the unconscious are not constrained by logic or language, but

are characterized by the free mobility of associative connections.

4. In addition, there are no negatives, partials, or contradictions in the unconscious. Unconscious mental functioning is thus more childlike, primitive, and operates according to the Pleasure Principle: wanting whatever it wants immediately without waiting or any substitutes.

Question: Is there any way of demonstrating these differences in conscious and unconscious mental activities?

Answer: The following hypnotic experiment illustrates some of these differences:

CASE REPORT:

Students were asked to make up a story based on the numbers 63359801. They found great difficulty in doing so and took five to ten minutes to come up with their stories, which were not very imaginative and tended to use the numbers concretely to indicate the numbers of various objects in their stories. Then the students were hypnotized and given the same instructions. The experimenter waited just three seconds before awakening the subjects. The following is an example of a story reported by one of the students after the hypnotically induced unconscious state: "There was an old German smoking a meerschaum pipe— the kind that curves downward into a bowl [shaped like the number 6]. He then pulled the pipe apart into two pieces [two parts of 6 = two 3s]. He then put the two parts of the pipe back together and placed the mouthpiece of the pipe against the heel of his hand [which produces an image roughly similar to the number 5]. Next, he turned the pipe upside down [the shape of the number 9]. The old German then used his pipe to trace the sign of infinity in the air [the number 8], and said, 'This is an experiment about mental powers, which extend from nothing [zero] to unity' [the number 1]."

Note how rapidly and ingeniously the student's mind created this narrative and set of images—in only three seconds, essentially the same length of time that it takes to produce a complex dream. It seems likely, in fact, that the images reported by the subject probably constituted a hypnotically induced dream.

Question: What is the relationship between depth psychologies and psychodynamics?

Answer: Another important feature of depth psychologies, which serves as a guiding concept of clinical interpretation, is the concept of psychodynamics. As in other disciplines, a dynamic perspective refers to conceptualizing phenomena in terms of an interplay of forces that oppose and balance each other. Clinical interpretation draws on this concept, for example, in its search for inner conflicts underlying patients' symptoms, for example, forces such as pleasure seeking or destructive drives counterbalanced by opposing feelings such as anxiety, guilt, and shame.

Question: What is the relationship of depth psychologies and clinical interpretation to the causes of psychopathology?

Answer: In addition to its psychodynamic viewpoint, depth psychologies also include a deterministic perspective, which underlies our interpretive attempts to understand the causes of psychological phenomena. Psychic determinism is divided into predisposing and precipitating causes. Even strange and bizarre behavioral phenomena are psychically determined. The deterministic aspect of mental events gives rise, for example, to the depth-psychological aphorism that "There is no such thing as a random thought"—a heuristic that serves as a guiding concept of clinical interpretation.

Question: What is meant by an interpretive heuristic?

Answer: In clinical and scientific work, heuristics are loosely systematic concepts and procedures that further inquiry and give good results on the whole, but do not guarantee them in any particular instance.

Question: Are there other basic concepts of depth psychologies that serve to guide clinical interpretation?

Answer: Another background assumption of depth psychology and guiding concept of clinical interpretation is the importance of childhood experiences. The role of this concept is related to that of psychic determinism, for childhood experiences are important predisposing causes (determinants) of all later behavior. Thus another aphorism of depth psychologies is that "Neuroses are made in childhood."

Question: Does this mean that clinical interpretations regularly emphasize connections between present psychological phenomena and early life experiences?

Answer: No. In general, communications of interpretations to patients dealing with childhood experiences are more possible and effective relatively late in the therapeutic process, when the therapist and patient have learned a great deal more about the patient's childhood experiences than was known earlier in the treatment.

Question: What keeps (childhood and other) traumatic experiences from being remembered?

Answer: Here again we encounter a psychodynamic balance of forces within the mind, this time between disturbing memories, fantasies, and inner conflicts on the one hand, and an opposing set of forces that attempt to avoid the pain of remembering by keeping the disturbing feelings and memories repressed. Sometimes, however, the inner feelings cannot be repressed completely, but begin to leak out in the form of symptoms. Thus, psychoneurotic symptoms are viewed as a disguised "return of the repressed." Depth psychologists also conceive of symptoms in this sense as *compromise formations,* that is, compromises that include both sides of opposing, conflicting forces in the mind.

Question: What are the principal forms in which the repressed can "return"?

Answer: The repressed can "return" in two principal ways: (1) massive breakdown of repression, with extensive "herniation" of the unconscious into the preconscious and consciousness, which produces psychosis, and (2) a "slow leak" of repressed material from the unconscious. Some such "leaks" produce quite normal phenomena, such as dreams, slips, jokes, sublimations in art, literature, and music, among others, which are normal outlets for unconscious fantasies and conflicts. Compare the aphorism that "Good men dream of what bad men do." Other, more extensive leaks may produce psychoneurotic symptoms, personality disorders, somatization reactions, and other effects.

Question: How do the preceding concepts relate to the purpose of mental functioning, including the purpose of symptoms?

Answer: The preceding discussion suggests another important concept of psychodynamics and clinical interpretation—that symptoms serve a purpose in the functioning of the mind. For example, the following clinical vignette (Seitz, 1953, pp. 405–409) illustrates what may happen when the purpose served by a neurotic symptom is removed hypnotically:

CASE REPORT:

During a series of clinical studies in which I was investigating the substitution of symptoms by hypnosis, a 41-year-old man was referred by a neurologist who had begun to suspect that the patient's coarse tremor of the hands and forearms might be due to hysteria rather than to postencephalitic parkinsonism. He had developed the tremor two years previously and could remember no unusual emotional disturbance associated with onset of the symptom. He claimed that one day, while lying on a couch and thinking of nothing in particular, his hands and arms began trembling. The presenting symptom was a rapid, coarse jerking of the hands and forearms in an oblique direction from above and near his body to downward and away from his body. The frequency of the tremor was approximately five times a second. His hands were held in a half-flexed, grasping position. No "pill rolling" of the thumb and fingers was present.

The first three times that the symptom was removed hynotically, the following spontaneous substitute symptoms occurred:

1. torticollis ("wry neck"), with his head twisted far to the left;
2. gagging, choking, and vomiting; and
3. a "bursting pressure" in his head.

Only one further attempt was made to remove the symptom hypnotically, for reasons that will be apparent. Following the trance, the tremor was absent, and, as had been suggested, the previous substitute symptoms also did not occur. This time the patient exhibited a dazed facial expression posthypnotically. He shook his head a few

13

times as if to clear it, then arose from his chair and advanced toward me. His hands were outstretched in a grasping position toward my throat. I rehypnotized him quickly (in studies of this kind, patients are trained to enter a trance at the count of three), and told him to go back and sit down, which he did. My final hypnotic instructions to him were that when he awakened he would have the tremor, but that through talk therapy with me he would find healthier solutions to the problems that had given rise to his symptom.

Q**uestion:**   What was the ultimate outcome of this case?

A**nswer:**

Case Report:

Dynamic psychotherapy with the patient led eventually to an abreaction of memories and emotions associated with an experience that occurred the day preceding onset of his tremor. The incident involved a fight with his boss.

In a fit of anger, his boss had called him a "son of a bitch" and a "motherfucker." The patient then lost control and tried to strangle the man. He was prevented from killing his boss by other employees. The next day his tremor began. Following the recovery of the precipitating event and working through of his inner conflict (both in the present and with regard to its childhood antecedents), he improved steadily and at the time of discharge was symptom free.

Question: Are there other ways in which the mind tries to avoid disturbing inner feelings and conflicts besides repression?

Answer: Yes. There are a number of further mental mechanisms, in addition to repression, for avoiding painful self-knowledge. Repression is the first line of defense against disturbing self-knowledge, but a number of other mental mechanisms are employed in concert with repression. Some of these, like denial, displacement, projection, and rationalization, reinforce repression. Others (e.g., sublimations) provide substitute outlets for repressed conflicts. Still other mechanisms simultaneously bolster repression and provide substitute outlets. For example, reaction formations keep disturbing unconscious feelings concealed not only by reinforcing repression, but also by doing the opposite of the disturbing unconscious fantasy or impulse. An example of reaction formation would be repression of unconscious conflict about latent hostile feelings, reinforced by the opposite attitude of behaving very politely toward the object of the hostility. To provide a margin of safety against the possibility of the latent hostility emerging into consciousness or action, defense mechanisms tend to be overdone; thus, another guiding concept of clinical interpretation is that "Excessiveness implies defense."

Question: How do interpretations produce change in patients?

Answer: Skeptics often ask how can just talking to patients, as in clinical interpretation, produce changes in them and cure or ameliorate some forms of psychopathology? One answer is: the same way psychological events change any form of behavior—namely, that people learn from experience. Therapy sessions are experiences that leave memory traces in the patient's brain. Psychological treatments therefore change not only the patient's mind and behavior, but also the patient's brain, through changes in the memory structure of their brains. Clinical interpretations build in new memories of the patient's therapeutic experiences and build down the patient's old traumatic memories and pathological ways of dealing with them.

Another way of describing such brain changes is in terms of neurotransmitters. For example, a 1998 study in Finland found, on the basis of brain-imaging studies, that a patient with borderline personality and mild depression who received a year of dynamic psychotherapy developed improvement in serotonin uptake in the medial prefrontal area of the brain, whereas a patient with the same diagnosis who did not receive psychotherapy continued to show abnormally low serotonin uptake in that area of the brain.

Question: Can such changes occur with brief therapy?

Answer: Despite all of the talk nowadays about "brief" therapies—talk that emanates largely from managed care companies whose profits are increased by short-term treatments—psychological treatments, by their nature, tend to take a relatively long time. Why is that? The answer, once again, has to do with the memory traces and brain changes mentioned before. Cognitive scientists have found that the learning of any complex subject—

math, chess, medicine, psychiatry, psychoanalysis, self-knowledge—requires many years of concentrated study. There is no short cut. That is simply one of the limitations of human cognitive functioning. It takes a long time to master complex subjects and also to unlearn old patterns. Two of the main reasons for this are: (1) the sheer amount of material involved in such learning and (2) constraints on the rate at which new information can be processed, assimilated, and stored (e.g., working memory can retain only about seven items of information at a given time).

Q**uestion:** Is there any other reason that psychological treatments take a relatively long time?

A**nswer:** Yes. In his volume *A History of Medical Psychology*, Gregory Zilboorg (1941, p. 6) referred to Dr. Johann Weyer (1515–1588) as the true founder of modern psychiatry, for the following reason:

CASE REPORT:

Early in the sixteenth century, an "epidemic of convulsions" developed in a group of nuns at a convent. Dr. Weyer was asked to help with the problem. From his observations of the convulsions, Dr. Weyer noted what he called "the ignominious villainy of the libidinous movements," and also that after the attacks the nuns "would open their eyes with an expression of shame." On the basis of those clues he surmised that the nuns were suffering from some kind of sexual conflict. He developed a method of treatment for them by sitting and talking with each nun individually for a long time. He found that for the nuns to confide openly, trust in him had to develop first. Eventually he learned that the hysterical convulsions originated when a group of young men had become acquainted with some of the nuns, following which they visited the nunnery at night and became increasingly intimate with them. The nuns, however, felt more and more guilty about their liaisons with the men and the inner fantasies and desires that the contact stimulated.

Question: From his clinical observations and interpretations, what discoveries did Johann Weyer make about this form of psychopathology (hysterical neurosis) and its treatment?

Answer: The following:

1. Inner conflict can be based on "forbidden" feelings and desires.
2. Disturbing inner conflicts may be concealed from oneself.
3. Under certain conditions, however, the conflict may break out of repression in disguised form as a symptom.
4. The symptom condenses both sides of the concealed conflict (in this case, for example, in the form of both the libidinous movements and the expressions of shame).
5. The role of the sexual drive exists in some forms of psychopathology.
6. Psychological treatment of such disorders requires that:
    a. First, rapport must be established between the patient and therapist, which may take a relatively long time.

b. The patient is encouraged to confide openly, which is difficult and takes still more time.

c. Clues in what the patient confides are used to interpret latent conflicts in the patient's mind.

RECAPITULATION

Clinical interpretation has been defined as a complex process of inquiry into the inner mental life of patients suffering from certain forms of psychopathology. It is a process because it involves a series of progressive and interdependent steps in order to attain its goal, which is primarily to gain information and understanding of the patient's inner mental life. It is a form of inquiry in the sense of investigation. *Inner mental life* refers to the importance of the unconscious in clinical interpretation.

The depth psychologies emphasize the importance of the unconscious in psychopathology and thus rely extensively on, and provide the following guiding concepts for, clinical interpretation:

1. A core feature of psychoneurotic pathology is a lack or avoidance of self-knowledge.
2. Depth psychologists maintain, by contrast, that it is both possible and useful for people to be in touch with their inner feelings and attitudes, even though such self-knowledge may cause discomfort.
3. Concerning the question of how much of the mind is unconscious, depth psychologists estimate that as much as seven-eighths of mental activities are unconscious.
4. Unlike preconscious mental activities, unconscious mental processes cannot be made conscious simply by focusing attention on them. For unconscious content to become conscious, specialized methods such as inference must be employed.

5. There is an emphasis on psychodynamics, that is, viewing phenomena from the standpoint of an interplay of forces in the mind that oppose and balance each other. Clinical interpretation draws on this concept, for example, in its search for disturbing conflicts underlying patients' symptoms.

6. A deterministic perspective, which attempts to understand the causes of psychological phenomena, is used.

7. Importance is placed on childhood experiences.

8. Repression and other defense mechanisms oppose consciousness of disturbing self-knowledge.

9. The concepts of neurotic symptoms are regarded as (1) a "return of the repressed," and (2) as "compromise formations" that condense both sides of an inner conflict.

REFERENCES

Fodor, J. (1983). Imagery and the language of thought. In J. Miller (Ed.), *States of mind* (pp. 85–86). New York: Pantheon.

Seitz, P. (1953). Experiments in the substitution of symptoms by hypnosis. *Psychosomatic Medicine, 15,* 405–424.

Whyte, L. (1960). *The unconscious before Freud.* New York: Basic Books.

Zilboorg, G. (1941). *A history of medical psychology.* New York: Norton.

Chapter 2

Collection and Observation of Clinical Data

Question: As Johann Weyer discovered over three centuries ago, one must first make the patient comfortable, facilitating the patient's rapport with, confidence in, and willingness to confide in the therapist. How is that done?

Answer:

1. By sincere interest in the patient and his or her problems.
2. By being natural and comfortable oneself.
3. By being tactful—not asking questions that might be too disturbing to the patient at first.
4. By answering the patient's questions honestly and relevantly.
5. By listening attentively and encouraging the patient's communication by nods of understanding and expressions like "I see."
6. By taking your time rather than being in a hurry to get through the session as quickly as possible.

7. By asking your questions and gathering information in a conversational manner rather than following a form or a standard list of questions.

Question: Does any data collection and observation occur during this beginning phase of the treatment?

Answer: The initial stages of both diagnostic and therapeutic interviews consist mainly of developing rapport, a process of "alliance building." Some important information for later clinical interpretations may be obtained during this phase, but that is not its primary aim. The ambience of this initial, rapport-building phase is a warm and interested process of getting acquainted with this new person and giving the patient a chance to get acquainted with you.

Question: How do you know when rapport is developing?

Answer: You can feel it—emanating from the patient and also within yourself—a relaxation and comfortable warmth of mutual interest and cooperation. Gradually, then, once such rapport has been established the sessions can become oriented more toward data gathering and interpretive inquiry. If at any point you sense the rapport declining, however—for example, from asking a question that is too disturbing or from going too fast—you must backtrack to more rapport building. The principle to follow in this regard is the same as Lord Beveridge's three words of advice to young investigators: "Gradualness, gradualness, gradualness!"

Question: When the diagnostic interviews are completed, you have recommended psychotherapy to the patient, and he or she has agreed to undertake therapy, how do you proceed from there?

Answer: By generating and gathering clinical data. Interpretive inquiry in the human and social sciences requires large amounts and wide varieties of data, partly because both interpersonal and intraindividual variability of phenomena in these fields is so much greater than in the physical sciences, and also because some of the best clues to latent meanings and determinants often depend on the recognition of relations and patterns (e.g., repetitions) in the data. The larger the number of data collected, therefore, the greater the chances of such relations and patterns appearing and becoming detectable in the data.

Question: What exactly is meant by "the clinical data"? What do they consist of?

Answer: What the patient says and does during the sessions, and what the therapist observes introspectively in his responses to the patient's associations. Everything else is inferred.

Question: How are clinical data generated and collected?

Answer: Clinical data are obtained in several ways: (1) free association by the patient, (2) the complementary method of "freely hovering attention" by the therapist, and (3) by observing the patient's behavior during sessions, including *how* the patient says and does what he or she says and does.

Question: When and how does the therapist explain the method of free association to the patient?

Answer: When the diagnostic interviews have been completed and the patient comes for his or her first therapy session, the therapist explains the method of free association to the patient in simple, easy to understand language, such as this:

CASE REPORT:

In treatments of this kind, it has been found useful for patients to relax, let their minds wander freely, and try to say everything that comes to mind. I will mainly listen, but from time to time will ask a question or call attention to something in your free associations that may call for closer study. At first you may find this method of talking difficult, but it will become easier and more natural with practice. There will be times when you think of something that you would rather not say because of embarrassment or concern about how you think I might react, but it is important for you to try to say it anyway. In fact, the harder it is for you to say, the more important it is for what we are trying to do in your treatment. At times questions will also come to your mind, and like everything else that occurs to you, go ahead and ask the question, but frequently I will not answer the question directly because answering questions directly is a conversation stopper, which we don't want to do, and because often it is more useful to inquire into your reason for asking a question—in that way learning more about what thoughts lie behind the question. Do you have any questions at this point about what I have just told you about the method of free association?

Question: Did Freud invent the method of free association?

Answer: Freud is usually credited with originating this method, but Francis Galton (1879–1880, p. 162) had described the method earlier and used it effectively on himself. Galton concluded that free associations "lay bare the foundations of man's thoughts with curious distinctness and exhibit his mental anatomy with more vividness and truth than he would probably care to publish to the world."

Question: What is the therapeutic rationale of free association? Why is it used so widely in depth-psychological therapies?

Answer: Rosner (1973, p. 558) explains the rationale of the process this way: "A thought presents itself to the patient. This thought stimulates another thought, which stimulates another thought (c,d,e . . . z). These thoughts are related to each other, each exerting an influence on succeeding thoughts. These thoughts proceed from the 'top down'—i.e., from the more ego-controlled to the less ego-controlled, from the more defended to the less defended, from the more conscious to the less conscious."

Question: Does free association carry over from one session to another?

Answer: Yes. Rosner (1973, p. 560) adds, for example, that "there is a connection between each succeeding session (if not in manifest, then in latent content). Thus the content, affects, and ideas from one session can be the stimulus for the idea that presents itself at the beginning of the next hour . . . A tension continues from one session to the next because of unfinished business to be continued or completed at the following session."

Question: Are there any other reasons that free association is so effective and useful in generating clinical data?

Answer: Yes. Another reason that free association is useful in depth-psychological therapies is the special (partially regressive, reverielike) state of mind that occurs when employing this method—as a result of which connections among thoughts are more extensively influenced by deeper mental processes than in ordinary states of consciousness.

Question: What reasons did Freud give for his emphasis on free association?

Answer: Freud (1925, pp. 40–42) claimed the following additional advantages for free association:

1. it provides an inexhaustible supply of data,
2. exposes the patient to the least amount of compulsion,
3. avoids the introduction of expectations by the analyst,
4. saves labor for both the patient and analyst,
5. maintains contact with the current situation, and
6. guarantees that no factor in the patient's neurosis would be overlooked.

Question: What does the complementary method of "freely hovering attention" by the therapist consist of, and what are its advantages?

Answer: Unfocused listening often makes it possible to "catch the drift" of the patient's latent thoughts. The therapist's evenly hovering attention involves a mental state of reverielike controlled regression (similar to the patient's), which facilitates experiencing events more as the patient experiences them. Freely hovering attention in a state of partial regression also involves a reduction of linear, discursive thinking, allowing the therapist to listen more openly, deeply, and nonlinearly to the patient's productions.

Question: How does the therapist's unfocused listening make meaningful connections with the patient's free associations?

Answer: Sooner or later the therapist's initially unfocused, passive–receptive mode of listening is disturbed by the intrusion of a thought, feeling, or fantasy image that the therapist notices (introspectively) because at first it seems to differ from what the patient had been saying. Soon after experiencing the response, however, the therapist may recognize a meaningful relation between the intruding content and the patient's associations. Freely hovering attention does not involve clearing the mind of thoughts or memories, but rather the capacity to allow all sorts of thoughts, daydreams, and associations to enter the therapist's consciousness while listening to the patient.

Question: If the therapist's listening is unfocused, isn't there a chance that he or she may miss something the patient says?

Answer: It is true that when we listen with evenly suspended attention we do not focus sharply on what the patient says; we half listen to the patient and half listen to our own reactions and associations. Thus, evenly distributed attention hovers between what comes from the patient and what comes from the therapist. Experimental studies suggest that evenly hovering attention seems to involve a process called listening away, or partial listening. Partial listening of that kind, however, appears to facilitate the perception and registration of subliminal stimuli, which have more direct access to preconscious and unconscious mental processes in the listener. The Gestalt concept of the "restructuring interval" also has some similarity to listening away; that is, insight often occurs when the clinician is not focusing on the immediate interpretive problem, as a result of which a spontaneous (preconscious), insightful restructuring of the problem may occur.

Question: Do therapists' listening strategies include anything other than freely hovering attention?

Answer: Yes. Listening in the depth psychologies is believed generally to be of a special kind—with the "third ear" as we sometimes say, and therapists do seem to listen more searchingly than anywhere else in life. There is something in our attitude, however, that goes beyond mere listening and passive availability. The silently listening therapist also conveys an implicit "demand" that transmits the message to continue talking, because there is more to learn about what is going on. The therapist's silence and patient waiting are thus an "expectant" form of listening, that is, an expectation that further associations will tend to clarify the patient's underlying problems.

Furthermore, passive free-floating attention is effective primarily when the patient's associations are relatively well organized rather than fragmentary. The more usual fragmentary nature of the material produced by free association often requires a more active, constructive (inferential) kind of listening. In addition, clinical listening is strongly influenced by the basic concept of continuity, which keeps us on the lookout for sequences, patterns, and coherence in the patient's associations. Other variations in listening include focusing alternatively on form and content, listening "to" versus listening "through" the patient's words, and listening "vertically" for hidden meanings as opposed to "horizontally" for repetitions of previous themes.

Question: Is therapeutic listening a process?

Answer: Definitely. As Freud (1923, p. 112) put it, often what one hears is not understood until later. For example, earlier

interpretations are progressively modified throughout the therapeutic process so that both the patient and therapist become
more alert and attuned to certain patterns in the patient's
associations. In addition, the patient gradually identifies with the
therapist's ways of listening, which promotes the development of
a capacity to listen to him- or herself with a more open mind (see
Chapter 7).

Question: What is meant by observing how the patient acts
and expresses his or her free associations?

Answer: This refers to paraverbal and nonverbal data. Paraverbal data include the prosodic features of tone, pitch, and melody,
rate and rhythm of speech, and variable smoothness of delivery.
Nonverbal data from the patient include posture, gait, gestures,
facial expressions, and repetitive movements.

Question: Are some types of clinical data more revealing of
unconscious mental processes than others?

Answer: The clinical literature contains many suggestions regarding specific types of data that individual investigators consider particularly revealing—the most noteworthy being Freud's
(1900, p. 168) reference to dreams as the "Royal Road" to the
unconscious. Some therapists believe that paraverbal and nonverbal data are even more revealing of underlying emotions and
conflicts than verbal data. The argument can be made, however,
that there is no *via reggia*, because all varieties of clinical data work

together to produce contextual meanings. It is not the dream alone, for example, but the timing, context, and manner in which the dream is told, the patient's extensive and varied associations to the dream, and the therapist's equally diverse responses to the associations, including inferences, that suggest its possible latent meanings and determinants.

RECAPITULATION

When the diagnostic interviews are completed, rapport has been established, and the patient has accepted the recommendation of psychotherapy, the treatment can become more oriented to data collection and interpretation. The need for large amounts and wide varieties of data are met by the patient's use of free association, the therapist's use of the complementary method of freely hovering attention, and observing how the patient speaks and acts.

The multiple advantages of employing free association include: providing an inexhaustible supply of data, exposing the patient to the least amount of compulsion, avoiding the introduction of expectations by the analyst, saving labor for both the patient and the analyst, maintaining contact with the actual current situation, and guaranteeing that no factor in the patient's neurosis is overlooked.

Some evidence suggests that evenly hovering attention by the therapist involves a process of "listening away," or partial listening. When we listen with evenly suspended attention we do not focus sharply on what the patient says; we half listen to the patient and half listen to our own reactions and associations. Thus, evenly distributed attention hovers between what comes from the patient and what comes from the therapist. Partial listening of that kind appears to facilitate the perception and registration of subliminal stimuli, which have more direct access to preconscious and unconscious mental processes in the listener.

31

Observing how the patient speaks and acts refers to paraverbal and nonverbal phenomena. It is questionable whether particular types of data are more revealing and clinically useful than others. All varieties of clinical data work together to produce contextual meanings. Despite Freud's contention that dreams are the "Royal Road" to the unconscious, it is not the dream alone, but the timing, context, and manner in which a dream is told, the patient's extensive and varied associations to the dream, and the therapist's equally diverse responses to the associations, including inferences, that suggest its possible latent meanings and determinants.

REFERENCES

Freud, S. (1900). The interpretation of dreams. *Standard edition*, 4 & 5. London: Hogarth, 1953, p. 608.

Freud, S. (1923). Remarks on the theory and practice of dream interpretation. *Standard edition* (Vol. 19, pp. 109–124). London: Hogarth, 1961.

Freud, S. (1925). An autobiographical study. *Standard edition* (Vol. 20, pp. 3–76). London: Hogarth, 1959.

Galton, F. (1879–1880). Psychometric experiments. *Brain*, 2, 149–162.

Rosner, S. (1973). On the nature of free association. *Journal of the American Psychoanalytic Association*, 21, 558–575.

Chapter 3

Data Processing

Question: What is the purpose of processing the clinical data?

Answer: To search for clues that can be transformed into latent meanings and determinants.

Question: Does this phase of the interpretive process have any similarity to methods in general science?

Answer: Yes. The scientific philosopher Hans Reichenbach (1951) commented on this phase of scientific inquiry:

> Knowledge begins with observation: our senses tell us what exists outside our bodies. But we are not satisfied with what we observe; we want to know more, to inquire into things that we do not observe directly. We reach this objective by means of

thought operations, which connect the observational data and account for them in terms of unobserved things.

Question: In clinical interpretation, what do we call the "thought operations" that Reichenbach refers to?

Answer: Cognitive processing and cognitive transformations.

Question: Does the term *cognitive* in this connection mean simply thought processes?

Answer: No. The scope of the term *cognitive* is much broader than just thought processes. Holt (1964, p. 650) writes that the term *cognitive* comprises "perceiving, judging, forming concepts, learning (especially that of a meaningful, verbal kind), imagining, fantasying, imaging, creating, and solving problems"—in other words, "all aspects of symbolic behavior, in the broad sense."

Question: Does the need for cognitive processing of the clinical data imply that depth-psychological understanding does not and cannot come about from direct perception of or close attunement to unconscious meanings and determinants?

Answer: Yes. Depth-psychological understanding is achieved by an indirect process of inferring "unobserved things" from our diverse clinical data.

Question: What is an example of "inferring unobserved things" in a physical science?

Answer: The inferential leap that is involved when a chemist no longer refers to the color of litmus paper but to orbiting electrons in the atomic structure of a substance and the displacement of electrons in the orbits (Klimovsky, 1991).

Question: Are there "rules" of data processing in clinical interpretation?

Answer: No. A rule-governed approach to data processing would restrict the kinds of inferences that could be made. Flexibility in data processing is necessary to increase the range of inferences that can be made in clinical interpretation so that the inferences can apply to the specific problem of a particular patient at a given time.

Question: But wouldn't a flexible approach that can generate any number and variety of inferences result in more frequent incorrect interpretations?

Answer: Yes, but speakers and listeners are accustomed to making some incorrect inferences and then correcting them as additional information is acquired.

Question: What is the basic modus operandi of data processing?

Answer: In the data-processing phase of clinical interpretation, selected clinical data and information from both patient and therapist are subjected to multiple, complexly interrelated data-processing operations that transform the data and information into unique personal meanings and determinants that are specific to the individual patient. These transformative operations are the pivotal axis of the interpretive process.

Question: Does the ability to carry out such processing operations require high general intelligence (IQ)?

Answer: The general cognitive requirements for therapists to carry out clinical data processing appear to be a special kind of intelligence called psychological mindedness. Isaacs (1939) illustrated this capacity long ago with the story of a five-year-old boy who said that "he didn't like dreams—they are horrid"; then, after a pause, he added, "and another thing—I don't have any!" Isaacs maintained that anyone with "psychological mindedness" immediately understands the boy's denial and concludes that because his dreams are horrid he wishes he didn't have any.

Question: What are the various cognitive operations employed in the processing of clinical data?

Answer: Some of the numerous operations employed in the processing of clinical data include contextualization, pattern seeking, thematization, restructuring, reversal, visualization, fractionation, abstraction, deconstruction, classification, completion, imagination, intuition, and inference. These and other methods of data processing are usually combined with each other rather than operating singly. Close study further reveals that even individual processing strategies are actually compound operations.

Question: What is the most frequent and important strategy of clinical data processing?

Answer: The most frequent and important clinical processing strategy is use of context. Freud (1900) recognized early in the development of psychoanalysis that correct interpretation can be arrived at only from the context at the time. Regarding the importance of context, he appeared to have been strongly influenced by Hughlings Jackson's view that context is "everything," that words in sentences lose their individual meanings.

Question: What is an example of contextualization?

Answer: Perhaps the most frequent form is the relation of the particular material of a here-and-now therapy session with what occurred in the preceding session or sessions. Another frequent form is the enrichment of a patient's material by related information from the therapist's associations, which include previous interpretations during the treatment as well as general knowledge. It is important to note, however, that although context is necessary to understanding, at times it can be biasing and misleading.

Question: What are some of the other most important data-processing operations?

Answer: Some other highly important data-processing methods employed frequently in the depth psychologies include *pattern seeking, thematization,* and *inference.* Although these operations can be discussed separately, it is important to keep in mind that in actual practice they function together.

Question: Isn't pattern seeking employed widely in general science?

Answer: Yes. The methodologist Abraham Kaplan (1964, p. 332) describes two principal ways of achieving understanding in science—either by fitting something into a known pattern or deducing it from other known truths. An example of pattern seeking in general science is Isaac Newton's observation of the "likeness between the thrown apple and the moon sailing majestically in the sky. A most improbable likeness, but one which turned out to be (if you will forgive the phrase) enormously fruitful" (Bronowski, 1978).

Question: Is contextualization a form of pattern seeking?

Answer: Yes. For example, when the therapist compares the here-and-now material of a session with recent sessions, he or she is looking for something that might connect the two. In clinical data processing, pattern seeking does not ignore the context from which the pattern was drawn. On the contrary, nearly all such cognitive processing is carried out with constant reference to the phenomena they describe.

Question: What are some of the common varieties of patterns that occur in clinical data?

Answer: Repetition of themes, analogical similarities, contiguities, and contrasts are among the most frequent types of relational patterns that clinicians identify in data processing and construction. They provide heuristic guides to which data are most relevant and suggest how to construe (construct) the latent meanings of those data. A corollary heuristic of pattern finding suggests that the larger the pattern the better; for example, the narrative strategy of data processing attempts to identify a coherent, storylike structure that encompasses essentially all of the clinical data.

Question: Is any one of the various types of patterns more frequent and important than the others in processing clinical data?

Answer: Neil Cheshire (1975, p. 113) considers analogical similarities the mainstay of pattern matching in clinical work and in data processing generally. As important as analogical similarities are in cognitive processing, however, they are not the sine qua non of data processing. They are just one pattern-seeking heuristic. For example, the following vignette by Ramzy (1974) illustrates both analogic amd repetitive patterns:

CASE REPORT:

At a time when a separation from the analyst was imminent, the patient became intensely disturbed about the possibility of losing his cleaning lady. Ramzy suspected that the patient's acute disturbance about losing his cleaning lady was a displacement from deeper concern about the coming separation from him. He based that surmise on having observed and construed similar such reactions in the patient when previous separations had occurred—a repetitive pattern—and also on a pattern of suggestive analogical parallels between the cleaning woman and the therapist: that is, both were in the paid service of the patient; both carried out personal services for the patient; and both seemed to be leaving him.

Question: What is thematization?

Answer: Thematization refers to the concept that a dynamic theme runs like an undercurrent through all of the data at a given time, for example, within a specific therapy session or over a series of sessions. This strategy is closely related to pattern seeking, the pattern in this case being sequential. Freud (1923) observed, for example, that the patient's associations tend to emerge as "allusions to one particular theme"; and John Klauber (1980, p. 196) noted that therapists routinely and actively search for a thematic pattern that gives "interdependent relevance" to everything the patient says.

Question: Is thematization something that the therapist applies to the clinical data, or does the patient also contribute to this phenomenon?

Answer: Both the patient and the therapist employ thematizing methods in different but reciprocal ways. The "productive" processing that underlies the patient's free associations includes a thematizing mechanism; and the therapist's listening, or "receptive," processing also is guided by a strategy of alertness to an underlying self-referential theme in the patient's discourse. Although the patient's conscious interest focuses at times on the therapist, the patient him- or herself is the central figure in most of the associations. The therapist thus tries not to initiate themes, but follows the patient's lead.

Question: How does thematization affect the interpretive process?

Answer: Thematization as a heuristic of cognitive processing makes the understanding of clinical material both easier and more difficult—easier because it reduces the "search space" for latent meanings and determinants to the principal dynamic theme at a particular time, but more difficult because the dominant theme of a therapy session is the most intensely defended against and its disclosure is the most tenaciously resisted. In addition, thematization implies that not just any construction can be considered acceptable, because it postulates that only one set of meanings and determinants—the dominant dynamic theme of a therapy session—can be considered the most plausible interpretation at a given time.

Question: Is the thematizing heuristic ever misused in data processing?

Answer: Yes. Like any generally useful data-processing heuristic, the search for thematic unity in clinical data can be misused; for example, doctrinal interpretation may be imposed on the data but rationalized as a unifying theme. In this regard, Meehl (1983, p. 360) offers the perceptive metaphor that "We want the [therapist] to *discern* the 'red thread,' not to spin it and weave it in." Doctrinal interpretations often betray themselves by accounting for only a few suggestive elements of the clinical data while ignoring the rest. Ideally, clinical interpretations are not based on the theories of any particular psychotherapeutic school, but represent an open-minded inquiry into latent meanings and determinants that are part of a unique, complex, momentary truth about a specific patient at a given time.

Question: What is a clinical illustration of thematization?

Answer:

CASE REPORT:

A young man came for treatment because of difficulty in sustaining relationships with women. After about two years of analytically oriented therapy he suddenly announced that he had become engaged to a woman he had dated for only a few months. I doubted (silently) that he had adequately resolved his conflicts about a close and sustained relationship with a woman, but rather than expressing the doubts I decided to wait and see what developed.

Soon after the engagement he began an appointment by extolling the "joys of marriage" and indicating how lucky he felt that Beth had accepted his proposal. His associations continued along those lines so effusively that I commented, "You sound very certain about your future with Beth. Do you ever have any doubts about it, or wonder whether there are any problems that might arise?" He seemed surprised by my question but his initial gush of associations began to slow down, and at that point he remembered a dream from the previous night. It was: "I was escaping from prison in Nashville, and was trying to escape to Memphis."

His associations to Nashville were about a former girlfriend, Betty, who lived in Nashville and from whom he had "escaped" because she "smothered him with love." He paused for a moment, then interjected that his present fiance, Beth, "is also very loving." His associations to Memphis were about Elvis Presley, who came from that city. He admired Presley for his fame, fortune, and especially his free-loving lifestyle. He sometimes imitated Presley as a joke. Recently he teased Beth that they should go to Memphis for their honeymoon and visit the Elvis Presley museum. (I asked about his associations to escaping from prison.) He recalled with a trace of embarrassment that he had told the dream to Beth, who was upset by it. She thought it meant that he felt imprisoned by their engagement and wished to escape. He protested to her that he had no such feeling, that the dream was about a former girlfriend from whose "clutches" he had escaped. Beth remained uneasy, however, and became even more disturbed when soon afterward he made a slip and called her Betty.

Question: What is the theme that runs through this entire session?

Answer: The issue of the patient's engagement—more specifically, his unacknowledged ambivalence about the engagement and coming marriage.

Question: What are the most prominent defense mechanisms against this thematic conflict in the session?

Answer:
  1. The suddenness of his engagement to a woman he had dated for only a few months—genuine "structural" changes

occur only slowly during treatment, whereas sudden changes are usually defensive—sometimes called a "flight into health."

2. The effusiveness with which he extolled the "joys of marriage" and how lucky he felt that Beth had accepted his proposal. The excessiveness of these associations suggested that they represented a defensive protest against doubts about the engagement and prospective marriage.

3. Displacement of his current situation, conflict, and ambivalence about engagement and marriage to Beth to Betty, a former girlfriend from whose "clutches he had escaped."

4. Joking, teasing Beth about, and imitating Elvis Presley. Thinly disguised, somewhat hostile, not so subtle ways of expressing his ambivalence and "Elvis wannabe" fantasies.

5. In the dream substituting his escape from prison in Nashville for his wish to escape from Beth.

6. His slip in calling Beth "Betty" is not so much a defense as a brief breakdown of the preceding defenses, but his protest and disavowal of its latent meaning were defenses.

Question: Why is inference so important in clinical data processing?

Answer: More than a century and a half before Freud, Christian von Wolff (1679–1752) wrote: "Insofar as something further exists in us than we are conscious of, we must bring it to life by *inferences* from that of which we are conscious, since otherwise we should have no ground to do so" (Whyte, 1960, p. 102).

Question: What is meant by *backward inference?*

Answer: The clinician first looks backward to discover determinants of present behavior, using "backward inference" to connect prior causes with current observable effects. Backward inference depends on skills of construction, that is, causal thinking that includes hypothesis formation and change, linking variables in causal chains, assessing the strength of such chains, and considering alternative explanations.

Question: Can clinical inference be employed by itself?

Answer: No. Inferring latent entities in clinical data should not be thought of as a separate or independent processing mechanism; it is merely one of a wide variety of interrelated cognitive transformations employed in interpretive processing, the combined operations of which help the therapist and patient to identify inner conflicts and defenses that need to be derepressed, channeled into talk, and understood more thoroughly and deeply in terms of childhood antecedents, emphasizing again that the interpretive process is concerned not only with latent meanings of mental events but also their unconscious determinants.

Question: Are clinical inferences relatively simple in form?

Answer: There is a tendency by clinicians to underestimate the complexities of the processes by which clinical inferences are made. The therapist's understanding necessarily depends on a very broad context of information about the patient that is built up only gradually over time, contributing eventually to better-informed and more effective inferences. Another aspect of inferential complexity is the therapist's use of dynamic reasoning in achieving understanding.

Question: Are most clinical inferences made consciously?

Answer: No. Most inferential processes are not reasoned out consciously or deliberately during the therapeutic process, but occur preconsciously.

Question: Are there different kinds of inferences?

Answer: Yes. Of the two principal types of inferences, inductive and deductive, most inferences in the interpretive process are inductive, which refers to reasoning from observational data (e.g., "I induce from the patient's scowl that he is displeased with me today"). Deductive inferences reason from the general to the particular. (For example, reasoning from the general heuristic that excessiveness implies defense, I deduce from the patient's overly aggressive protest that he may be feeling anxious.) The latter example actually includes both deductive and inductive inferences because the observation of the patient's overly aggressive reaction is a form of clinical data.

Question: What is an illustration of clinical inference?

Answer:

CASE REPORT:

The case of the "Elvis wannabe" presented in the section on thematization also includes a key inference based on the following set of clues: his "protesting too much" about how lucky and happy he felt about his engagement; the contrast between that attitude and the dream of escaping from prison, which he associated with escape from a previous woman who was overloving toward him; contiguity of that association with the thought that his new fiance is also very loving; the dream image of escaping to Memphis, which he associated with Elvis Presley, whom he admired especially for his free-loving lifestyle; his teasing Beth that they should go to Memphis for their honeymoon and visit the Elvis Presley museum; his telling the dream to Beth, denying that it referred to his relationship with her but then making a slip and calling her Betty. Putting all of these clues together, I inferred that he felt ambivalent about his sudden engagement but was trying very hard to conceal the ambivalence from himself.

RECAPITULATION

In the data-processing phase of clinical interpretation, selected clinical data and information from both the patient and therapist are subjected to multiple, complexly interrelated data-processing operations that transform the data and information into unique latent meanings and determinants that are specific to the individual patient. These transformative operations are the pivotal axis of the interpretive process.

Some of the most important cognitive transformations employed in the depth psychologies are contextualization, pattern seeking, thematization, and inference. A common form of contextualization is the comparison of current associations with the findings of recent sessions. Enrichment of a patient's material through related information from the therapist's associations is another common form of contextualization.

Repetition of themes, analogical similarities, contiguities, and contrasts are among the most frequent types of relational patterns that clinicians are alert to in data processing and construction. They provide heuristic guides to which data are most relevant and suggest how to construe (construct) the latent meanings of those data.

Thematization refers to the concept that a dynamic theme runs like an undercurrent through all of the data at a given time, for example, within a specific therapy session or over a series of sessions. This strategy is closely related to pattern seeking, the pattern in this case being sequential.

The processes by which clinical inferences are made are highly complex, often taking the form of dynamic reasoning. Students sometimes ask, "Do we really need such detailed knowledge of the preconscious processes that underlie our clinical interpretations? Will it make us better interpreters?" The short answer to that question is yes; the long answer tells why, namely: The more we can learn about methods of cognitive transformation and the more we are able to make that information part of our clinical, interpretive knowledge base, the more likely we are to draw on and use that knowledge preconsciously (intuitively) in the depth-psychological understanding of our patients.

REFERENCES

Bronowski, J. (1978). *The origin of knowledge and imagination* (pp. 109–110). New Haven, CT: Yale Universiy Press.

Cheshire, N. (1975). *The nature of psychodynamic interpretation.* London: Wiley.

Freud, S. (1900). The interpretation of dreams. *Standard edition,* 4 & 5. London: Hogarth, 1953, p. 98, fn. 1.

Freud, S. (1923). Two encyclopaedia articles. *Standard edition* (Vol. 18, pp. 235–262). London: Hogarth, 1955, p. 239.

Holt, R. (1964). The emergence of cognitive psychology. *Journal of the American Psychoanalytic Association, 12,* 650–665.

Isaacs, S. (1939). Criteria for interpretation. *International Journal of Psychoanalysis, 20,* 148–160.

Kaplan, A. (1964). *The conduct of inquiry* (p. 332). New York: Crowell.

Klauber, J. (1980). Formulating clinical interpretations in clinical psychoanalysis. *International Journal of Psychoanalysis, 61,* 195–201.

Klimovsky, G. (1991). Epistemological aspects of psychoanalytic interpretations. In H. Etchegoyen (Ed.), *The fundamentals of psychoanalytic technique* (pp. 471–493). London: Karnac Books.

Meehl, P. (1983). Subjectivity in psychoanalytic inference: The nagging persistence of Wilhelm Fliess's *Achensee* question. In J. Earman (Ed.), *Testing scientific theories* (pp. 346–411). Minneapolis: University of Minnesota Press.

Ramzy, I. (1974). How the mind of the psychoanalyst works: An essay on psychoanalytic inference. *International Journal of Psychoanalysis, 55,* 543–550.

Reichenbach, H. (1951). *The rise of scientific philosophy* (pp. 176–177). Berkeley: University of California Press.

Whyte, L. (1960). *The unconscious before Freud.* New York: Basic Books.

Chapter 4

Construction and Reconstruction

Question: What do the terms *construction* and *reconstruction* refer to in the interpretive process?

Answer: Freud (1937) used these terms interchangeably, but from the standpoint of the interpretive process it is useful to distinguish between constructions and reconstructions. Reconstructions deal primarily with crucial childhood events that have shaped the patient's personality and which, as Freud (1918) wrote, "are as a rule not reproduced as recollections, but have to be [interpreted] gradually and laboriously from an aggregate of indications." Constructions are not necessarily concerned exclusively with early life experiences, but often focus on current dynamic issues. In other interpretive disciplines, construction is defined as a relatively discrete phase of the construal process in which the interpreter attempts to formulate a tentative overall or "whole" (thematic) meaning of the current data being studied.

Question: How did Freud describe the method of construction?

Answer: In one of his encyclopaedia articles he stated (1923) that what the therapist listens for is the "drift," that is, the gist, essence, or theme of the patient's associations, that in favorable circumstances the undercurrent meanings emerge indirectly in the form of allusions, and that the allusions are to "one particular theme," of which the patient is unaware. The therapist then "guesses" the central theme or motif from the allusions in the patient's material.

Question: Does this mean that constructions are guesswork?

Answer: Partially, yes, and it means that Freud recognized the conjectural aspect of constructions (cf. the "inductive leap" in the discovery process of science). Freud (1910) wrote also in this connection that it is impossible to give specific instructions about the method of arriving at a symbolic interpretation because "success must be a question of hitting on a clever idea, of direct intuition."

Question: What is meant by "a symbolic interpretation."

Answer: Symbolic relations define or treat one thing in terms of another. The highly developed symbolic function in humans conserves resources and storage of information by grouping comparable things together and interpreting new experiences according to representations of types, but the richly variegated possibilities of symbolic relations make them relatively error prone in interpretive processing.

Question: Is the conjectural aspect of constructions related to the uncertainty of interpretations?

Answer: Very much so. The necessity to guess initially about the overall meaning is a major factor in the uncertainty of interpretations.

Question: Is this conjectural factor specific to therapeutic discourse or does it also occur in other forms of communication?

Answer: It probably occurs in all forms of discourse. Compare, for example, the parallel with the psychology of ordinary communication (Miller, 1967, pp. 775–777):

> The listener begins with a guess about the input information, on the basis of which he or she generates a matching internal signal. The first guess is often wrong, which leads to another such guess. The cycle of guessing, mismatches, and corrected guesses recurs until a satisfactory match is obtained. The efficiency of this process depends largely on the quality of the initial guess. If the initial guess is close, the iterative process is completed rapidly; if not, the listener may not be able to keep up with the flow of speech. Initial guesses are like predictive hypotheses about what incoming messages will turn out to be.

Advance postulates make it possible to attune one's apperception to certain interpretations while rejecting others.

Question: In view of its conjectural aspect, can there be a correct model of construction?

Answer: No. The complexities, difficulties, and limitations of the clinical interpretive process are such that there can never be a method or model of correct construction, because the psychology of understanding cannot be reduced to a systematic procedure and there is no way of assuring a right "guess" by means of rules and principles.

Question: Does "guessing" in the constructive phase of interpretation have any relation to intuition?

Answer: Sometimes perhaps, but not consistently. Intuition is a mix of psychological constructs, including imagery and narrative formation, with an underlying basis of experience. It is nonlogical and gestalt in nature; is characterized by the suddenness, unexpectedness, associated affect, and ineffability of the insight; a relationship between intuition and creativity; and confidence in the process while at the same time realizing that an intuitive insight may be incorrect.

Question: What is the most necessary and useful reason for the use of conjecture in constructions?

Answer: Guesses about the underlying "whole" or thematic meaning of a given set of data are attempts to discover an explanation that can coherently tie together all of the data studied at that time. In casting about preconsciously and imaginatively in search of the best explanation, we consider various possibilities and choose the one that seems to account for the data most completely and coherently. This type of inferential reasoning (called abduction) is exploratory—a process of trying out various possible explanations, including quite novel ones, to account for the data as completely and coherently as possible. We do not simply apply some preexisting clinical theory to the data. Our preconscious operations are imaginative, original, and creative; they attempt to construct the best explanation of the data, whatever that may be, whether it is part of psychodynamic theory or not.

Question: So the conjectural aspect of construction relies to a considerable extent on the use of imagination?

Answer: Yes, and unfortunately some therapists underestimate the power of our imaginative capacities in cognitive processing and construction. In this connection, Andresen (1983, p. 142) cogently suggests that we should not look to Freud or the leaders of other therapeutic schools for all the answers, but should cultivate receptivity in therapy sessions and create our own low-level, first-order interpretive theories, for the best explanation of a given set of data may come from common sense rather than from one of our numerous clinical theories.

Question: Does this mean that one should try to be as free of preconceptions as possible?

Answer: Yes. Freud (1912) insisted, for example, that the most successful results occur when we allow ourselves to be surprised by any new developments in the data and respond to them with an open mind, as free of preconceptions as possible. He metaphorically suggested that in our interpretive work theory should remain like a stranger who has not been invited into the house. In other words, it is to a clinician's credit as an interpreter if he or she is open-minded and inventive enough to construct nondoctrinal explanations of our rich, ambiguous, overdetermined data.

Question: What other mental operations besides conjecture are involved in construction?

Answer: Construction draws on all of the mind's capacities, in particular a back-and-forth focus on parts and whole, which is the principal processing operation of hermeneutics. The thematic meaning of a therapy session corresponds with the "whole" meaning of hermeneutic theory. The "part" meanings are the individual data of the session. Part and whole meanings are interdependent; that is, the whole is derived from and constituted by the parts, the parts being delineated and integrated by the whole. Thus the thematic meaning of a therapy session ties together the meanings of all of the session's individual data. Freud (1911) employed the part–whole principle in his concept that the meaning of any fragment depends on the meaning of the whole. The meaning one seeks to understand, however, is grasped first in a tacit sense before it is known more fully.

Question: What is the role of coherence in constructions?

Answer: A central problem in understanding discourse is the issue of continuity, or "connectivity," within the data. The continuity is not manifest, however, so the interpreter must link data to other data. Coherence refers to the degree of internal consistency that a construction is able to impart to clinical data and their overdetermined meanings. As a criterion of internal consistency, coherence rests on its relation to the basic concept (background assumption) of continuity. That is, to the extent that a construction exhibits a potential for organizing meanings coherently, we assume that it reflects one of the most characteristic features of clinical data and of latent meanings themselves, namely, their continuity.

Question: Does this concept influence how one listens to clinical data?

Answer: Yes. Freud's view of the clinical process in this connection has significantly influenced the way we listen to patients: namely, our goal is to recognize the underlying thread of continuity in the patient's associations; thus we necessarily listen with an ear tuned to sequence and coherence.

Question: How is the concept of coherence actually applied in the constructive phase of the interpretive process?

Answer: The therapist scans the associations heuristically and notes which elements of the data "cohere" with each other in some manner, for example, by similarity, contrast, repetition, or sequence. Coherence becomes even more important once a tentative whole meaning (e.g., thematic conflict) has suggested itself to the therapist, for at that point the interpreter undertakes a more systematic review of the clinical material to determine whether the data as a whole fit together coherently in terms of the initial construction. The gradual shaping of a more definitive construction depends even further on coherence—to assess the "goodness of fit" produced by each trial revision of the construction. The adequacy of the final construction is assessed by its ability to integrate the individual data and meanings of the entire session into a coherent whole.

Question: Is coherence involved in the checking and justification of constructions?

Answer: Yes (see Chapter 5), but its use differs in these two phases of the interpretive process. For purposes of construction, it is not necessary to account for all of the data, some of which are not even available yet. The degree of internal consistency needed at this stage is only a rough approximation between a tentative hypothesis and the major, most evident meanings of the clinical data. At this point even very rough equivalences such as posited analogical patterns may be "good enough" for the purposes at hand. When used for purposes of justification, however, the criterion of coherence is applied to all of the data, with particular attention to how all of the details (the individual associations and their part meanings) fit together, and how they fit with the thematic or whole meaning represented by the construction.

Question: What is an example of construction?

Answer:

CASE REPORT:

In the case of the "Elvis wannabe" (see Chapter 3), on the basis of multiple clues, I constructed that he was ambivalent about his sudden engagement to Beth but was trying hard to conceal the ambivalence both from Beth and himself. In the case of the man who was so disturbed about the possibility of losing his cleaning lady (also in Chapter 3), Ramzy constructed that the patient's disturbance was about a coming separation from the therapist. He based that construction on the patient's reactions to previous separations from the therapist (a repetitive pattern), and on several analogical parallels between the functions of the cleaning lady and the therapist in the patient's life.

Question: What is an example of reconstruction?

Answer: Freud (1937) described a prototypical example of reconstruction in the following way: A reconstruction

> lays before the subject of the analysis a piece of his early history that he has forgotten, in some such way as this: Up to your nth year you regarded yourself as the sole and unlimited possessor of your mother; then came another baby and brought you grave disillusionment. Your mother left you for some time, and even after her reappearance she was never again devoted to you exclusively. Your feelings towards your

mother became ambivalent, your father gained a new importance to you . . . and so on.

Question: Are there any similarities between constructions and reconstructions?

Answer: Yes, there are a number of similarities between the two: For example, both employ the constructive strategy of imaginative "guessing" (i.e., since reconstructions do not replicate childhood experiences exactly, they necessarily involve a constructive aspect). Both must avoid the doctrinal fallacy of imposing specific clinical theories on the data, and both formulate alternative interpretive hypotheses that are then subjected to checking, revising, and rechecking in order to determine the most plausible interpretation at the time.

Question: Is it a mistake to base a reconstruction on a clincal theory or model of childhood development?

Answer: Arlow (1991, pp. 543–544) warns that reconstructions are particularly prone to doctrinal interpretation, that is, use of a specific genetic model of infantile psychology to guide reconstructions of a patient's associations. Examples include Klein's and Kohut's interpretive approaches, which are doctrinally driven by their respective theories of pathogenesis. Arlow refers to this type of reconstruction as "foisting upon the patient's associations an interpretation based upon a model concept of pathogenesis." Paniagua (1985, p. 323) notes that use of specific psychogenetic theories in interpretations all too easily becomes indoctrination.

Question: Is it possible to reconstruct accurately the traumatic memories from the patient's childhood?

Answer: Freud (1918) wrote that the patient's childhood experiences "are as a rule not reproduced as recollections, but have to be constructed gradually and laboriously from an aggregate of indications." In one of his final publications, however, he (1937) proposed that the therapeutic process is frequently unable to recover repressed traumatic experiences from childhood, but that a sense of conviction about the correctness of a reconstruction "achieves the same therapeutic result as a recaptured memory." A number of writers since Freud argue, however, that for depth-psychological therapies to make scientific as well as therapeutic claims, the criterion of interpretive (including reconstructive) accuracy must be retained.

Question: What is an example of reconstructing a specific, idiosyncratic childhood experience?

Answer:

CASE REPORT:

A middle-age professional man came for treatment because of a chronic psychosomatic gastrointestinal disorder. A long-standing marital problem emerged in the course of his therapy. He wanted more closeness with his wife, including tender physical contact and sexual intimacy, but she preferred a certain distance, separate bedrooms, and less sex. He had been brought up in a strict, stoic, discipline-oriented family in which emotional display of any kind was discouraged. Partly for that reason he had never been able to verbalize his frustrations to his wife; he assumed that she would find such complaints childish, demanding, and inappropriate. Repressed negative feelings toward his wife emerged slowly, painfully, and against considerable resistance. The latter included the rationalization that a mature person would rise above such feelings. Eventually, however, he became able to discuss the problem with his wife. She responded in her customary cool and detached manner, saying that they were close enough for her and that what he wanted seemed possessive to her. In reporting this interchange with his wife, he added, "Naturally, I dropped the matter after she said that." In subsequent associations he mentioned that he had developed a choking sensation in his throat during the past two days. He blocked for a minute, then recalled a childhood experience that had always puzzled him. The incident involved a summer-long separation from his family when he was 9 years old. He had been very homesick, eagerly awaiting his mother's return. When she arrived, however, rather than hurrying to meet her he fled, hiding himself so effectively that no one could find him for over an hour. Over the years he had thought about that incident many times but never understood why he ran away from his mother when he wanted so much to see and be with her.

I experienced a subjective reaction to his memories of the childhood incident, a slight constriction of my own throat, to which I associated a suppressed sob. I then recalled the patient's choking sensations following the discussion with his wife and also the highly rational, antiemotional family atmosphere in which he had grown up. Putting these several sources of information together I asked gently, "Were you afraid you might cry when you saw your mother?" The patient choked up suddenly and started to weep, but collected himself and said that of course that must have been the reason he fled—to hide his tears of relief at being reunited with his mother.

I then reminded him that he had been feeling choked up since the discussion with his wife. Tears came to his eyes again, but this time his jaw was set and his eyes blazed through the tears. He expressed hurt and anger about his wife's apparent indifference to what he had told her. When the anger began to subside I asked, "Can you see the parallel between hiding from your mother and 'dropping the matter' with your wife? Both reactions involved defensive avoidance, that is, withdrawing from a disturbing emotional confrontation." He could see the parallel but not its implication.

I explained that the tears he was afraid for his mother to see must also have been angry tears—anger at feeling alone and lonely for so long. He began to weep again, this time with sobbing, following which for the first time he expressed bitter feelings toward his mother for her apparent indifference to his loneliness and hurt as a child.

This example also includes some constructions as well as a reconstruction, which is often the case in the latter.

RECAPITULATION

Although Freud used the terms *construction* and *reconstruction* interchangeably, I have stressed certain distinctions between the two. Constructions are not necessarily concerned exclusively with early life experiences but also deal with current pathodynamic issues, and according to traditional (hermeneutic) usage in other interpretive disciplines, construction is defined as a relatively discrete phase of the construal process in which the interpreter attempts to formulate a tentative overall, or "whole," (thematic) meaning of the current data being studied. Reconstruction, by contrast, is a gradual process in which crucial childhood events are not reproduced as recollections, but have to be constructed gradually from diverse data.

Construction draws on all of the mind's capacities, in particular a back-and-forth focus on parts and whole, which is the principal processing operation of hermeneutics. The whole (thematic) meaning is derived from and constituted by the parts, the latter being delineated and integrated by the whole. Freud employed the part–whole principle in his concept that the meaning of any fragment depends on the meaning of the whole. The whole meaning one seeks to understand is grasped first in a tacit sense before it is known more fully.

The complexities, difficulties, and limitations of the interpretive process are such that there can never be a method or model of correct construction because the psychology of understanding cannot be reduced to a systematic procedure and there is no way of assuring a right "guess" by means of rules and principles.

Guesses about the underlying "whole" or thematic meaning of a given set of data are attempts to discover (construct) an explanation that can coherently tie together all of the data studied at that time. In casting about preconsciously and imaginatively in search of the best explanation, we consider various possibilities and choose the one that seems to account for the data most completely and coherently. Our goal is to find an underlying thread of continuity in the patient's associations; thus we necessarily listen with an ear tuned to sequence and coherence.

We do not simply apply some preexisting clinical theory to the data, which would be a doctrinal fallacy. Rather, our preconscious data-processing and constructive operations are imaginative, original, and creative. They attempt to construct the best explanation of the data, whatever that may be, whether it is part of psychodynamic theory or not. Thus we should not look to Freud or the leaders of other therapeutic schools for all of the answers, but should cultivate receptivity in therapy sessions and create our own low-level, first-order interpretive theories.

REFERENCES

Andresen, J. (1983). Guided tours or lonely searches [Review of the book *Dire mastery: Discipleship from Freud to Lacan*]. *Contemporary Psychiatry, 2,* 141–142, p.142.

Arlow, J. (1991). Methodology and reconstruction. *Psychoanalytic Quarterly, 60,* 539–563.

Freud, S. (1910). The antithetical meaning of primal words. *Standard edition* (Vol. 11, pp. 153–162). London: Hogarth, 1957, p. 97.

Freud, S. (1911). The handling of dream-interpretation in psychoanalysis. *Standard edition* (Vol. 12, pp. 89–96). London: Hogarth, 1958, p. 93.

Freud, S. (1912). Recommendations to physicians practising psychoanalysis. *Standard edition* (Vol. 12, pp. 109–120). London: Hogarth, 1958, pp. 112, 114.

Freud, S. (1918). From the history of an infantile neurosis. *Standard edition* (Vol. 17, pp. 3–122). London: Hogarth, 1957.

Freud, S. (1923). Two encyclopaedia articles. *Standard edition* (Vol. 18, pp. 235–262). London: Hogarth, 1955, pp. 238–239.

Freud, S. (1937). Constructions in analysis. *Standard edition* (Vol. 23, pp. 255–270). London: Hogarth, 1964.

Miller, G. (1967). *The psychology of communication.* New York: Basic Books.

Paniagua, C. (1985). A methodological approach to surface material. *International Review of Psychoanalysis, 12,* 311–325.

Chapter 5

Checking the Correctness of Interpretations

Question: What are the principal limitations of our interpretive methods that make checking and rechecking of constructions necessary?

Answer: The principal limitation is that the grounding of our interpretations is neither scientific law, a nomic universal, formal theoretical structure, nor even purely observed fact, but largely a shifting, ever unfolding context of interpreted events. Tuckett (1994, p. 869) notes, for example, that "interpretations rest on interpretations, rest on interpretations, rest on interpretations, etc." Thus there is always an element of uncertainty in every possible aspect of interpretation, which Hirsch (1967, p. 322) maintains is a defining feature of interpretation.

Question: Do these limitations and uncertainties make errors inevitable in our interpretive work?

Answer: Yes, not only inevitable but frequent. Clinical interpretation is not "easy" and "trustworthy in every respect," as Freud claimed, but is difficult and fallible. Even the language we use to discover, construct, formulate, and justify latent mental processes limits as well as facilitates what can be perceived and understood in patients' associations; for language, including paralinguistic and nonverbal cues, serves purposes of concealment as well as expression. In addition, every person draws differently from the repertory of verbal, paraverbal, and nonverbal devices.

Question: Do these problems have a counterpart in general science?

Answer: Yes. The preceding problems are examples of so-called method effects in scientific inquiry; that is, the methods we use decisively influence and constrain what we can observe and understand. The methods one uses to solve a scientific (including interpretive) problem are thus an important part of the problem itself.

Question: Do present-day therapists realize that Freud overestimated the reliability of clinical interpretation?

Answer: Unfortunately, Freud's view that interpretation is "easy" and "trustworthy" persists in a widespread tendency by clinicians to underestimate the difficulties and fallibility of our interpretive methods. I. A. Richards (cited in Hirsch, 1967) insisted, by contrast, that "the only proper attitude toward a successful interpretation is to view it as a triumph against odds," and Kermode (1979, p. 125) wryly observes that interpretation is an "impossible but necessary" task.

Question: What needs to be done about this problem?

Answer: "Damage control," that is, systematic use of error-detecting, error-correcting, and justifying procedures, needs to become an accepted and regular part of the interpretive process. To deal with errors realistically, one must attempt to recognize mistakes when they occur and, if possible, put them to some use in the interpretive process. For example, we attempt to recognize and utilize countertransference phenomena as potential aids to understanding, and the same basic error-correcting strategy of learning from one's limitations and mistakes applies to all types of clinical errors. At its best, clinical interpretation is a process in which mistakes are put to good use.

Question: Is there more than one type of checking and justifying procedure?

Answer: Yes. It is necessary to distinguish between checking activities *during* therapy sessions and more definitive justification after the completion of treatment. The former consists mainly of attempting to determine the most plausible alternative constructions at a given time. More definitive justification of clinical interpretations requires additional posttherapeutic investigation based on a record of the entire (completed) therapeutic process, which the therapist or investigator can study retrospectively and systematically in as much detail as necessary. The latter, more extended and detailed justifying process, can also employ multiple, increasingly exacting justifying procedures, including microanalytic methods of studying the clinical data (for detailed descriptions and illustrations of these methods, see Rubovits-Seitz [1998, pp. 211-281]).

Question: What do error-detection strategies involve?

Answer: Error detection begins with the expectation that one will make mistakes. That mind-set increases the clinician's alertness to discrepancies between his or her constructions on the one hand, and all of the clinical data (rather than selected data that support one's hypothesis) on the other. The clinician who accepts the inevitability of errors doubts everything that goes into his proof: his facts, his hypotheses, and whether the two fit together as he thinks they do.

Question: Does this attitude have parallels in general science?

Answer: Yes, scientific skepticism. Acceptance of errors and recognition of discrepancies are crucial strategies not only in clinical work but in all scientific and interpretive activities. Darwin (1888, p. 83) wrote, for example, that he could not recall a single hypothesis that did not have to be modified or abandoned eventually. Gordon's (1982, pp. 13–14) description of deciphering ancient scripts also emphasizes the importance of recognizing errors. Decipherers make inferences that seem to fit some pattern inherent in the text, but the inferences may or may not be correct. Such guesses are necessary, but most of them are wrong. Wrong guesses are exposed as incorrect by the fact that they lead to impossible combinations when applied elsewhere in the text. Guesses must be made, but for every correct guess, many wrong ones must be scrapped. Thus, a prime quality of the scientist, the cryptanalyst, and the clinical interpreter is flexibility.

Question: What is meant by error-correcting strategies?

Answer: Error-correcting strategies comprise a process of continuous, increasingly exacting evaluations of clinical interpretations. Because constructions are essentially conjectures about the "whole" (thematic) meaning of the data being interpreted, the interpreter (1) checks how much of the data a construction accounts for, (2) modifies the construction to account for more of the data, and then (3) rechecks the revised construction to determine whether it now covers most of the data. If not, the interpreter must consider discarding the original construction and replacing it with a different hypothesis. The process of checking, revising, and rechecking constructions usually results in several promising modified hypotheses.

Question: If the interpreter has several promising alternate constructions, how does he or she choose among them?

Answer: The principal selection criterion at this phase of the justifying process is internal evidence, that is, which of the alternate hypotheses accounts for the largest number of data most consistently, coherently, and comprehensively. At this point in the error-correcting process, the clinician has selected what appears to be the "most plausible" interpretive hypothesis from among various competing constructions.

Question: Are there any further error-correcting procedures?

Answer: During the actual therapeutic process itself, this is essentially as far as the error-correcting process goes. An additional phase of the error-correcting process includes justifying procedures, only some of which can be employed during the course of treatment. Other, more definitive justifying methods must await a record of the completed treatment.

Question: What does posttherapeutic justification involve?

Answer: The posttherapeutic phase of interpretive justification requires a record of a completed therapeutic process, which can be studied in as much detail as necessary. Systematic, retrospective study based on the record of a completed treatment employs more varied, complex, detailed, and probative methods of justification. Like the interpretive process as a whole, the justification of interpretations is pluralistic. The most probative methods of justifying interpretations include cross-validation and convergence of evidence, demonstration of organized interlocking microstructures underlying interpretations, indirect prediction and postdiction (of classes of events), and repetition of themes and patterns.

Question: What about the widely used methods of coherence and patients' responses to interpretations?

Answer: Those methods are less reliable, especially if used alone—coherence because it is circular, and patients' reactions because the patient's responses themselves must be interpreted. When these methods operate in concert with other, more probative justifying methods, however, cross-checking of their results can occur. Quantitative methods, including computer-assisted content analysis, also have a place in posttherapeutic investigations of the therapeutic process. Qualitative and quantitative methods can be combined advantageously for both process analysis and the justification of interpretations (for accessible descriptions of these various justifying methods, see Rubovits-Seitz [1998, pp. 211-248]).

Question: How are interpretations justified posttherapeutically?

Answer: Freud's concepts and strategies of interpretive justification included or anticipated a number of methods employed in contemporary human and social science methodologies. One of the prescient aspects of Freud's justifying approach, for example, was its pluralism. Human and social science methodologies build redundancy into their justifying checks as a substitute for the infallibility of individual methods. Multiple checks reduce errors, and two proofs are better than one. Freud's justifying approach included:

1. The use of internal evidence, mainly coherence, encompassing the vast network of observations and interpretations from the entire therapeutic process;
2. All of the various (mainly indirect) responses to interpretations—remission of symptoms representing only one such response;
3. Postdiction;
4. The prediction of similar findings in other cases;
5. External validation.

The pluralistic nature of Freud's justifying approach also includes the potential for cross-validation based on multiple samples and varieties of clinical data drawn from many episodes and phases of the therapeutic process, and convergence of evidence from diverse justifying methods.

In addition, Freud's (1923) jigsaw puzzle model of interpretive justification anticipated the importance of small-scale, microstructural evidence in the justification of interpretations, that is, the complex interrelations of part meanings associated with individual elements of the clinical data. Freud insisted, for example, that "Our presentation begins to be conclusive only with the intimate detail" (Nunberg & Federn, 1962, p. 172). Edelson (1984, pp. 136–137) writes similarly that the emergence of circumstantial detail having a high degree of specificity and idiosyncratic nuance should be given special weight in reports of fantasies, experiences, and other data. It is these data, Edelson continues, that in the end prove to be the most relevant to the search for probative evidence.

Question: What is an example of checking and justifying a construction?

Answer: This example draws once again on the case of the "Elvis wannabe" (Chapter 3). To review the case briefly:

CASE REPORT:

The patient, who had problems sustaining relationships with women, announced suddenly and relatively early in his treatment that he had become engaged to his present girlfriend, Beth. When he extolled the "joys of marriage" effusively, I commented that he seemed very certain about how the relationship with Beth would work out—did he have any doubts about it? He then recalled a dream in which he "escaped from prison in Memphis, and tried to escape to Nashville." His associations to prison in Memphis were about a former girlfriend, Betty, who lived there and "from whose clutches he had escaped," because she "smothered him with love." He paused and added reflectively that "Beth is very loving, too." His associations to Nashville were about Elvis Presley, whom he admired and sometimes imitated because of his "fame, fortune, and free-loving lifestyle." He had joked to Beth that they should go to Nashville for their honeymoon and visit the Elvis

Presley museum. He mentioned with embarrassment that he had told the dream to Beth, who was upset by it. She thought it meant that he felt imprisoned by his relationship with her, which he protested was not the case. But Beth remained uneasy, especially when he made a slip and called her Betty.

My construction of this session's material was: latent ambivalence about the engagement versus not wanting Beth to know about his ambivalence (possibly out of guilt toward her).

Question: How might one justify this construction during the patient's treatment?

Answer: By checking how well the construction integrates all of the session's associations, including the dream images.

Question: Can the effusive inital associations about the "joys of marriage" be explained by the construction, and if so, how?

Answer: Yes. By the dynamic heuristic that "Excessiveness implies defense." He protested too much about it—a defense.

Question: Can the construction account for his reaction of surprise and slowing down the effusive associations when I asked whether he ever had any doubts about his future with Beth, and if so how?

Answer: Yes. These reactions appeared to fit the posited dynamic theme as a momentary weakening of the overcompensatory defense.

Question: Does the construction account for his suddenly recalling a dream from the previous night?

Answer: Yes. By virtue of the interpretive heuristic that weakening of a defense produces changes in the form or content of associations, which may include the recall of "forgotten" material such as a dream.

Question: How can the construction account for the dream, including the term *escape* twice?

Answer: The repetition fits the posited dynamic theme as a hoped-for solution to his underlying conflict; that is, he had managed to escape from a previously confining relationship with Betty, which appeared to serve as a basis for hoping that he might be able to escape again, this time from Beth.

Question: What is the significance of his mentioning that Betty "smothered him with love," followed immediately by the reflective thought that Beth is also very loving?

Answer: By these associations to the dream, he unwittingly equated Betty and Beth by the contiguity of his references to the two women, which fits the posited thematic conflict that he wants to get away from Beth, as he did from Betty.

Question: Does the dream imagery of escaping from confinement in prison support the dynamic theme, and if so how?

Answer: Yes, by its analogy with a confining relationship, which Beth herself sensed when he told her the dream. The prison metaphor also could imply guilt, suggesting that he may have been continuing his relationship with Beth in part because of some pressure from his conscience to fulfill his commitment to her.

Question: Does the dream statement that he was "trying to escape to Nashville" fit the dynamic theme of ambivalence about the engagement?

Answer: Yes. That dream image elicited associations about his imitation of Elvis and admiration of his "free-loving lifestyle," which fits the dynamic theme of hoping to return to his own free-loving bachelorhood.

Question: Did the patient's embarrassment on recalling that he had told the dream to Beth, and that she was upset by it, fit the dynamic theme of the session?

Answer: Yes, by its quality of his feeling "caught in the act"—in this case caught in the unacknowledged fantasy—of wishing he could get out of the engagement and marriage.

Question: What about his denial to Beth that the dream had anything to do with her?

Answer: A disavowal defense.

Question: Does his slip in calling Beth "Betty" fit the theme?

Answer: Yes. Despite his denial to Beth, his slip in calling her "Betty" provided still further support for the posited thematic conflict.

Since all of the data from the reported session have been accounted for coherently by the dynamic theme of ambivalence about the engagement, we are justified (at least partially and tentatively) in considering the posited construction the most plausible interpretation at the time of that session.

Question: Can one consider constructions that are checked and corrected during the therapeutic process to be firmly justified?

Answer: No. Constructions and reconstructions always involve a selection and progressive modification of an initially plausible interpretation, the justification of which is relative at every stage of the therapeutic process. The numerous revisions and reshaping of constructions, and the filling in of reconstructions, result from two main features of the interpretive process: (1) the gradual weakening of defenses, with the consequent emergence of further information from previously repressed memories and mental processes; and (2) the detection and correction of previous interpretive errors in the case.

RECAPITULATION

The correctness of our interpretations is unavoidably limited because their grounding is neither scientific law, a nomic universal, formal theoretical structure, nor even purely observed fact, but is largely a shifting, ever unfolding context of interpreted events: Interpretations rest on interpretations, rest on interpretations, rest on interpretations, etc. Thus there is always an element of uncertainty in every possible aspect of interpretation, which must be considered a defining feature of interpretation.

The limitations and uncertainties of the interpretive process make errors inevitable and frequent in our clinical interpretive work. For these and other reasons, clinical interpretation is not "easy" and "trustworthy in every respect," as Freud claimed, but is difficult and fallible. Freud's view that interpretation is "easy" and "trustworthy" persists, however, in a widespread tendency by clinicians to underestimate the difficulties and fallibility of our interpretive methods.

"Damage control" is a more realistic attitude toward the interpretive process, that is, systematic use of error-detecting, error-correcting, and justifying procedures. To deal with errors realistically one must attempt to recognize mistakes when they occur and, if possible, put them to some use in the interpretive process.

Error detection begins with the expectation that one will make mistakes. That mind-set increases the clinician's alertness to discrepancies between his or her constructions on the one hand, and all of the clinical data (rather than selected data that support one's hypothesis) on the other.

Error-correcting strategies comprise a process of continuous, increasingly exacting evaluations of clinical interpretations. Because constructions are essentially conjectures about the "whole" (thematic) meaning of the data being interpreted, the interpreter checks how much of the data a construction accounts for, modifies the construction to account for more of the data, and then rechecks the revised construction to determine whether it now covers most of the data. If the revised construction does not account for most of the data, the interpreter must consider discarding the original construction and replacing it with a different hypothesis.

The clinician selects what appears to be the most plausible interpretive hypothesis from among various competing constructions, based on which hypothesis can account for the data most coherently and comprehensively. An additional phase of the error-correcting process includes justifying procedures, only some of which can be employed during the course of a treatment. Other, more definitive justifying methods must await a record of the completed treatment, which can be studied posttherapeutically in as much detail as necessary, employing multiple, increasingly exacting methods of justification.

REFERENCES

Darwin, C. (1888). *The life and letters of Charles Darwin.* New York: Basic Books.

Edelson, M. (1984). *Hypothesis and evidence in psychoanalysis.* Chicago: University of Chicago Press.

Freud, S. (1923). Remarks on the theory and practice of dream interpretation. *Standard edition* (Vol. 19, pp. 109–124). London: Hogarth, 1961, p. 116.

Gordon, C. (1982). *Forgotten scripts.* New York: Basic Books.

Hirsch, E. (1967). *Validity in interpretation.* New Haven, CT: Yale University Press.

Kermode, F. (1979). *The genesis of secrecy: On the interpretation of narrative.* Cambridge, MA: Harvard University Press.

Nunberg, H., & Federn, E. (Eds.). (1962). *Minutes of the Vienna Psychoanalytic Society* (Vol. 1, p. 172). New York: International Universities Press.

Rubovits-Seitz, P. (1998). *Depth-psychological understanding: The methodologic grounding of clinical interpretations.* Hillsdale, NJ: Analytic Press.

Tuckett, D. (1994). The conceptualization and communication of clinical facts in psychoanalysis: Forward. *International Journal of Psychoanalysis, 75,* 865–870.

Chapter 6

Communicating Interpretations to the Patient

Question: What is the process of communicating interpretation to patients called?

Answer: The criteria and methods of communicating depth-psychological information to patients are referred to as interpretive technique. A vast literature has accumulated on the subject and problems of interpretive technique, while much less attention has been paid to our methods of seeking, construing, formulating, and attempting to justify latent meanings and determinants (for the latter, see Rubovits-Seitz, 1998).

Question: What was Freud's rationale for communicating depth-psychological information to patients?

Answer: He wrote (1910) that the continued existence of neurotic structures depends on their distortion, which prevents their recognition by the patient. When the riddle they present is solved, communicated to, and accepted by the patient, they no longer are able to exist, which he compared with "evil spirits whose power is broken as soon as you can tell them their name—the name which they have kept secret."

To the doubts of critics that anything can be done about neurotic illness by merely talking, Freud (1916–1917) argued that "Words were originally magic and to this day words have retained much of their ancient magical power . . . Words provoke affects and are in general the means of mutual influence" between people.

Question: Did he actually believe the analogies about "evil spirits," "breaking their spell," and the magical powers of words in communications to patients?

Answer: No, those were just analogies not meant to be taken literally. Later (1915c) he wrote, for example, that "A moment's reflection shows that the identity of the information given to the patient with his repressed memory is only apparent. To have heard something and to have experienced something are in their psychological nature two quite different things, even though the content of both is the same." Still later (1916–1917) he wrote:

> *Our* knowledge of what is unconscious in the patient is not equivalent to *his* knowledge of it; if we communicate our knowledge to him, he does not receive it *instead of* his unconscious material, but *beside* it; and that makes very little

change in it . . . The repression must be got rid of—after which the substitution of the conscious material for the unconscious can proceed smoothly. (Italics are Freud's)

Question: What did he propose in order to deal with these problems of communications to patients?

Answer: He (1915b) proposed the further technical concept of "working through":

> The first step in overcoming the resistance is made . . . by the analyst's uncovering the resistance, which is never recognized by the patient, and acquainting him with it . . . [But] one must allow the patient time to become more conversant with the resistance with which he has now become acquainted, to *work through* it, by continuing, in defiance of it, the analytic work according to the fundamental rule of psychoanalysis.

Question: What are the principal issues of interpretive technique?

Answer:
1. Verbal reformulation of interpretive hypotheses;
2. Whether (and why) to communicate interpretations;
3. What (including how much) to communicate;
4. When to communicate;
5. How to communicate interpretations.

Question: Why is verbal reformulation of interpretations necessary?

Answer: Because prior to their verbal reformulation, clinical experiences are registered mentally by the therapist in a basically ambiguous form. Reformulating the raw material into language gives it structure, organizing it along specific communicable lines. Even during the listening phase of the interpretive process the clinician's aim is not only to receive information and to maintain contact, but also to prepare for the communication of interpretations to the patient.

Question: Into what form of language is the interpretation reformulated?

Answer: Since the therapist's aim is to convey depth-psychological information that will be understandable and useful to the patient, not just any language will do for verbal reformulation. Thus, consideration must be given to what kind of language would best convey the therapist's interpretive impressions. The choice of language to be used is guided by multiple factors, including the dynamics of the therapeutic process at that particular time; previous experiences with the patient that suggest the kinds of language to which he or she is most responsive; use of simple, nontheoretical language, including the patient's own words and metaphors when possible; and the additional criteria discussed below, namely, whether (and why), what (and how much), when, and how to communicate interpretations.

Question: What issues are involved in the question of whether (and why) to communicate an interpretation?

Answer: Considerable controversy exists concerning this question. Many therapists believe that the most important criterion for deciding whether to interpret is the development of resistance that interferes with the progress of therapy. Kleinian analysts, however, who communicate interpretations more frequently than therapists of other schools, base their decision of whether (and why) to interpret on the appearance of anxiety in the patient. Melanie Klein stressed that interpretations should be based on the patient's anxiety level (the "point of urgency"). She felt that the patient's point of urgency obliges the therapist to interpret without delay (Etchegoyen, 1989, p. 342).

Still another group of writers emphasizes the importance of spontaneity in communicating interpretations. They argue that truly creative interpretations are often not only bold but also surprise those who make them; thus it is not unusual for us to realize what we have said to the patient only after we have expressed it.

Question: What are the issues involved in what (and how much) to interpret?

Answer: The content of what is interpreted varies, of course, depending on the dynamics of the therapeutic process at a particular moment. Thomas M. French (1958) stressed the value of attempting to thematize and understand what he called the "focal conflict" at a particular time: "The therapist should not be content with fragmentary bits of insight. His constant aim should be to understand how different trends and themes in the patient's associations fit together into a single intelligible context." He applied the same clinical principle to the technique of communicating interpretations to patients and suggested that therapists interpret to patients at the level of the focal conflict (French, 1963, pp. 212–213):

> Interpreting the focal conflict often activates it more intensely and centers the patient's reaction even more sharply on the analyst and on what the analyst said . . . [whereas] if the analyst should interpret some conflict which at the moment is at the periphery of the patient's interest, then the effect may be to activate a competing focus and thus to make the patient's [responses to the interpretation] much more difficult to understand.

The various therapeutic schools differ most on how much to interpret—an issue that for the therapist involves conflict between interpreting and keeping silent. Freud was very active; he asked questions, illustrated his assertions with quotations from Shakespeare, and made comparisons. Lacan (1968), on the other hand, compared the analyst with the dummy in bridge. Most therapists appear to agree, however, that whatever one interprets should be as brief and to the point as possible, in contrast to rambling communications.

Question: What are the main issues in the question of when to interpret?

Answer: Regarding the timing of interpretations, Loewenstein (1958) emphasized that it be "at the right moment," when the patient is "ready to receive it." He acknowledged, however, that it is difficult to define when that moment occurs. Many therapists apppear to believe that the right moment is when resistance interferes with the flow of associations.

Question: What are the issues involved in how to interpret?

Answer: Although Freud did not follow these recommendations consistently, he discouraged bringing one's own individuality into the relationship and interpretations. He argued against "educational activity" and cautioned about intellectual discussions. He also cautioned the clinician "not to rush." In his paper on "transference love," (1915a) he again emphasized the necessity to carry out the treatment in abstinence, but added: "I do not mean physical abstinence alone, *nor yet the deprivation of everything that the patient desires, for perhaps no sick person could tolerate this*" (emphasis added). Here Freud slightly opened the door to some important changes in technique that have developed since his death. (Kernberg, 1988, has presented a recent synthesizing review of post-Freudian developments in technique.)

Question: What changes have occurred in the role of abstinence?

Answer: Around the middle of the twentieth century, at about the same time that the scope of indications for depth-psychological therapies widened gradually, overuse of abstinence began to diminish in the treatment of more disturbed patients who, in order to tolerate the anxiety and frustrations of the therapeutic situation, often require warmer, more "human" responses from the analyst.

Question: What other changes have occurred?

Answer: A related development that began at around the middle of the twentieth century was growing interest in counter-transference phenomena. Studies of this issue have been pursued further by numerous investigators. As Theodore Jacobs (1999, pp. 180–182) observes, this aspect of therapeutic technique actually has origins in Anna Freud's (1954) caveat that therapeutic "technique was not designed for the defense of the analyst" but enjoins the analyst to consider privately "all that passes within him for its informational value in terms of the patient." Jacobs continues, in this way "we are able to turn to the interactional level of analysis, not as an avoidance of depth psychology but with a fuller realization of the implications of unconscious functioning in each of the parties, each with his own unconscious." This approach is not concerned only with the words exchanged between patient and therapist, but with

> the underlying messages that accompanied these communica-
> tions . . . transmitted through tone and syntax, vocal quality
> and inflection, posture and movement . . . feelings, atti-
> tudes, and values of which neither patient nor [therapist] is
> consciously aware. This level of communication serves to
> modify, punctuate, emphasize, or contradict the words spoken
> by each.

Question: Has the interest in countertransference phenomena led to still other changes in technique?

Answer: The depth-psychological interactive perspective implicit in the wider use of countertransference in the interpretive process probably contributed, in turn, to the growth of interest in (object-)relational, intersubjective, and dialectical constructivist viewpoints. Kernberg (1988) integrates ego-psychological and object-relations theories.

Question: Does this include the more radical "relational approach" advocated by Greenberg and Mitchell (1983) and Mitchell (1997)?

Answer: No. A fundamental assumption of the latter approach is that *everything* in the therapeutic process can be cast in a relational perspective, focusing on the immediate therapeutic interaction. It elevates an exclusive interpersonal perspective over any intrapersonal considerations. Many clinicians argue, however, that the relational element, even if not made explicit, has always been part of psychoanalytic and dynamic psychotherapeutic practice, and in a recent publication Greenberg (2001) criticizes the relational approach that he helped to develop (see also Chapter 13).

Question: What is meant by an intersubjective approach to therapeutic technique?

91

Answer: An intersubjective approach emphasizes the dyadic, collaborative nature of the therapeutic relationship, including candid expressions of feedback—even if these involve very negative feelings—between the two participants. It views psychoanalysis and dynamic psychotherapy as two-person psychologies and questions the traditional objective and authoritative position of the analyst in one-body (intrapsychic) theories such as Freud's. Where the classical paradigm emphasizes the therapist's objectivity and the patient's transference, the intersubjective approach recognizes that transference and countertransference inevitably commingle. The intersubjective approach differs also from the objectivist paradigm by emphasizing and confirming the patient's point of view through dialogue and some self-disclosure by the therapist (see Chapter 12).

Question: Is there such a thing as a pluralistic approach to therapeutic technique?

Answer: Yes. Therapists who are pluralistically inclined attempt to employ both traditional and intersubjective models; they try to identify clinical situations in which it is best to interpret transference, and others in which it is better to engage in dialogue. At times, however, the two paradigms can become confused, in which case the intersubjective approach may lead to transference–countertransference enactments (see Chapter 14).

Question: What is the status of self-disclosure (by the therapist) in therapeutic technique?

Answer: Jacobs (1999, pp. 180–182) has reviewed the history of self-disclosure in psychoanalysis and dynamic psychotherapy, and evaluates whether it is an error or an advance in therapeutic technique. He concludes that most depth-psychological therapists consider it questionable; but although it cannot be prescribed at this time as a general technique, further clinical experience with self-disclosure may reveal that in selected cases and clinical situations it may be found useful.

Question: What is the "dialectical constructivist" approach?

Answer: The dialectical constructivist approach, associated mainly with the writings of Irwin Z. Hoffman (1994, 1998), proposes a theory of therapeutic and interpretive action that emphasizes "spontaneity" and "self-expression" (though not the degree of self-disclosure used in the intersubjective approach); but at the same time he stresses that the therapist's effectiveness is enhanced also by adherence to certain psychodynamic "rituals," including abstinence and the asymmetrical aspect of the therapeutic relationship. He refers to this double demand on the therapist's functioning as "struggling to find an optimal position relative to the dialectic between formal [clinical] authority and personal responsivity and self-expression." He (1994) concludes that "some acceptance by the patient of the recognizably technical aspects of the analyst's behavior is essential," and notes that:

> Classical technique, especially when practiced in a rigid way, is a familar target of criticism for its seeming coldness. I would say it is actually a scapegoat, a whipping boy, for a problem that cuts across most of the major theoretical positions . . . It is more difficult but equally important to locate the

expression of [problems] in points of view that advertise themselves explicitly as warmer or more "human" alternatives to the classical position. Self psychology is one such point of view. The central principle of technique in self psychology is "sustained empathic inquiry." Can conformity to such a "benign" principle cast a shadow . . . on the analyst? I think it can. (Hoffman, 1994, p. 191)

Question: What is an example of dialectical constructivism in therapeutic technique?

Answer: Hoffman (1994, p. 197) cites an example of what he considers an excellent example of dialectical thinking in an account by Mitchell (1988) of the optimal posture of a therapist for dealing with narcissistic issues in the transference. Mitchell (1988, p. 205) presented the following example of a patient seeking a "mutually admiring relationship" with the therapist:

> Responding to such [a narcissistic transference] in a way that is [therapeutically] constructive is tricky, and difficult to capture in a single formula. What is useful most frequently is not the words, but the tone in which they are spoken. The most useful response entails a dialectic between joining the analysand in the narcissistic integration and simultaneously questioning the nature and purpose of that integration— both a playful participation in the analysand's illusions and a puzzled curiosity about how and why they came to be so serious, the sine qua non of the analysand's sense of security and involvement with others.

Question: What is Hoffman's position on openness, self-disclosure, and the uncertainty of the interpretive process?

Answer: Hoffman (1994, p. 215) concludes that the therapeutic and interpretive attitudes that are "most integrative and authentic must be an alloy of doubt and openness . . . the work requires an underlying tolerance of uncertainty and with it a radical, yet critical kind of openness that is conveyed over time in various ways, including a readiness to soul-search, to negotiate, and to change." In this connection, Meissner (2001, p. 192) suggests that what we need and seek

> is a theory of the self as an *open* system—but if we are to have an open system, it should be a system that continues to maintain its own inherent organization, structure, stability, coherence, constancy, identity and integrity. If we open such a system to the influence of others in the form of relatedness, intimacy, attachment and affiliation, we do not have to destroy it in the process.

Question: What is a clinical illustration of communicating interpretations to the patient?

Answer:

CASE REPORT:

Karen was a 33-year-old married woman whose treatment began in a psychiatric hospital following a suicide attempt. She had taken a moderate overdose of tranquilizing drugs prescribed by her family physician. She was cooperative, only mildly depressed, and talked freely about a problem with her husband. His work required a great deal of travel, to which she had adjusted during their six years of marriage. In recent months, however, even when he was not traveling he often worked late at his office, not coming home until midnight. She had complained mildly to him about her loneliness, but he was not very sympathetic. In an interview with him at the hospital, he confided to me that he no longer found Karen interesting or attractive, but remained married to her from a sense of duty. He denied any extramarital involvement.

Karen was intelligent, sensitive, and related well during her sessions with me. Her physical health had always been good, and she had no history of previous mental illness. She was devoted to her husband, who encouraged her own career in art. She had a small circle of friends with whom she visited regularly, but she spent most of her time working alone in her home studio. She loved her work and home, did not want children, and except for seeing so little of her husband was generally satisfied with her life.

Karen's father had left her mother when Karen was only 2 years old. She never saw or heard from him after that and had no memory of him. Because her mother had to work to support the family, Karen and her older brother were left alone a great deal. Her brother resented having to look after his little sister, which he expressed by ignoring her. Between the ages of 6 and 16 she had looked forward to each summer, which she and her brother spent with their grandparents in another city. Her brother found other boys to play with during those summers, but there were no girls in the grandparents' neighborhood for Karen. Therefore, for the most part, she spent the time with her grandparents, who were very fond of her and she of them. Her grandmother was an invalid, but her grandfather was a kindly, good-natured, energetic man who became the companion, playmate, and "father" that Karen had never had.

Karen's twice-weekly dynamic psychotherapy began while she was in the hospital and continued for three years on an office basis. The initial phase of her treatment focused on the problem with her husband. Eventually she confided that she felt not only lonely but sexually frustrated. Earlier in their marriage she and her husband had enjoyed frequent, passionate, and exciting varieties of sexual relations, but he no longer seemed interested in sex. She continued to desire sex, partly for its own sake, but also because sexual relations were important to her self-esteem and to maintaining a feeling of closeness to her husband.

As the therapeutic process continued and deepened, she reported dreams that combined the image of her husband with that of her brother, who had ignored and neglected her during childhood. She now recognized that her suicide attempt had been motivated by anger at her husband and hope that it would force him to be more involved with her. She recalled similar self-destructive attempts to gain her brother's sympathy and attention during childhood.

Early in the second year of her therapy, her feelings toward me became increasingly positive, idealizing me in much the same way that she had felt about her grandfather. During the weeks preceding the session to be interpreted, her dream imagery became increasingly erotic in character and her fantasies included intense, pleasurable expectations that I would erotically respond to her sexual feelings. (I raised the question of whether she might be reexperiencing feelings toward me that she had felt toward her grandfather.) She then confided that her close and loving relationship with her grandfather had included frequent genital fondling of each other during the time she was 7 to 13 years old. She seemed relatively free of conscious guilt or shame about the sexual contact with him. She had rationalized to herself that she was entitled to the pleasure it gave her because she had been deprived of a father's and a brother's love, and because she had received so little time and attention from her mother.

The feelings she described for her grandfather had both the quality and intensity of romantic love (Jones, 1938; Fenichel, 1945, p. 98). From the beginning of their mutual fondling she had been the one who always initiated the sexual intimacy. Whenever she felt lonely for her mother or rejected by her brother during those summers, she would look for her grandfather, cuddle up to him, fondle his penis or place his hand on her genitalia, which would lead to five or ten minutes of mutual genital fondling. She stopped having sexual contact with her grandfather when she was 13 years old, which she associated with the onset of her menses. From then on, rather than seek erotic contact with her grandfather, she masturbated while recalling and fantasizing about her previous sexual experiences with him. Even as an adult her most exciting and satisfying erotic fantasies were based on pleasurable memories of sexual contact with her grandfather.

Confiding the childhood sexual experiences with her grandfather did not immediately lessen Karen's increasingly romanticized feelings toward me. When I called attention to her coy and somewhat flirtatious behavior toward me, she readily admitted that she had a crush on me, that she envied my wife, imagined what it would be like to be married to me, and thought about me when she masturbated.

Appointment Preceding the Session to be Interpreted

During the phase of increasing erotic transference to me, Karen came in one day looking flushed and distraught, which was unusual for her. She blurted out that she was very upset about a cat in her neighborhood that had become pregnant. She went on at length about her concern for the animal and its pregnancy. When she began to calm down, I asked why she was so concerned about a normal condition like pregnancy? She replied with a tone of anxious pity that the cat was only a kitten and seemed much too small to carry and give birth to a whole litter of young. She recalled feeling awed by the size of pregnant women's distended abdomens. She was glad that neither she nor her husband wanted children because she would never want to feel like that.

Session to be Interpreted

Karen was still upset when she came for her next appointment. She started by saying in an anxious and slightly accusatory tone that the kitten was becoming gigantic—more distended every day. She continued talking about the pregnant kitten and its "plight" for some time. When her feelings of alarm had peaked and began to decline, I asked her exactly what was she afraid might happen. She replied that she was "desperately afraid" that the kitten's abdomen would become so distended from the babies inside that it would just burst, which would kill the poor kitten. She then recalled a dream from the previous night:

> I was driving a school bus, stopping along the way to pick up children. More and more children boarded the bus until there was no room for more. But more kept getting on, until finally children started flying out of the bus windows. I was terrified and didn't know what to do.

99

She had no idea what the dream might mean. She had never driven a school bus and had never been responsible for a group of children. The children were very young—nursery school or prekindergarten age. She recalled with surprise that she seemed to enjoy driving the school bus and picking up the children—until the bus began to get overcrowded. Then she felt terrified at what was happening and at her inability to stop it.

I asked, "Can you see a parallel between the overcrowded bus and the pregnant kitten?" She looked blank for a moment and then suddenly exclaimed, "Oh! Of course! So overcrowded with children that they 'burst out.' It's the same thing I've been afraid would happen to the kitten. So the school bus must represent the kitten." I commented, "But in the dream in was *your* school bus, and you were in the driver's seat, suggesting that the school bus refers to something about yourself and your body." Karen blinked unbelievingly, then protested that she wasn't pregnant, never had been, and never wanted to be. I reminded her that all kinds of strange things can go on in the unconscious—even disturbing dreams about pregnancy. "But I don't *want* to be pregnant," she insisted. She could never stand the idea of being "bloated with babies" and feared the process of giving birth. I asked, "What specifically do you fear about it?" She replied that she feared the pain, the bleeding, the possibility that she might hemorrhage and die, and she recalled a woman describing her birth canal being "ripped and torn" as the baby came out.

I then interpreted: "It is clear that you have a great deal of conflict about pregnancy and giving birth, but despite that conflict, when a woman loves a man very much, she may want to have his child." She responded, "Well, I love my husband, but I certainly don't want to have his child!" I said, "I understand that, but recently you said that you have a crush on me, that you envy my wife, and that you have wondered what it would be like to be married to me. Your romantic feelings toward me may include wishes to give me a child—or for me to give you a child."

Karen paused and became reflective at that point. A blush appeared as she said, "My daydreams about being married to you sometimes picture you coming home from your office to me and our children. In those daydreams, the children are already there. The thought of being pregnant with them and giving birth to them didn't occur to me." I then interpreted further: "This is probably not the first time you have experienced intense conflict about wanting to have a child with a man you loved. The same conflict may have occurred early in your marriage when you felt very romantically toward your husband. And I suspect that the conflict first occurred during your loving and erotic relationship with your grandfather. If so, that might help to explain why you are so fearful about pregnancy and giving birth. The fantasy or prospect of becoming pregnant while still a child could make a young girl feel the way you've been feeling lately about the pregnant kitten." Karen nodded slowly and thoughtfully.

Question: What was the principal current (thematic) conflict of this session?

Answer: The wish to have the therapist's (or grandfather's) child versus fear that her body (as a child) was not large enough to contain and give birth to a child, but might burst open and kill her.

Question: What was the precipitant of this conflict?

Answer: Her increasingly intense romantic–erotic grandfather transference to me.

Question: What were the principal defenses against the conflict?

Answer:
1. Repression and transference as defenses against remembering her feared childhood wishes for grandfather's child.
2. Disavowal of any wish for a child.
3. Projection of her conflict about pregnancy to the pregnant kitten and to the dream image of an overloaded school bus.

Question: What was the genetic antecedent of the thematic conflict?

Answer: Her intense, prolonged, romantic–erotic relationship with her grandfather, which appears to have included a highly conflicted wish for a child from him.

Communicative Strategies in the Illustrative Case

Question: What verbal transformations were employed?

Answer: Throughout much of the session I was searching for the right words to help the patient understand the projection of her own pregnancy fantasy to the kitten, and the relation of her pregnancy fantasy to me in the present and to her grandfather in childhood. As much as possible, I attempted to use words that she had expressed. To find such words, I raised a number of questions to elicit further information on exactly how she felt about what she was experiencing.

Question: How could the questions of whether (and how) to interpret be answered in this session?

Answer: The answer to both of these questions was that the patient's associations, dreams, and other material had become increasingly clear about their underlying meanings, and the patient herself was so close to grasping them that it would take only the slightest additional information to help her understand the latent meanings and determinants.

Question: What about the question of what (and how much) to interpret?

Answer: The most important strategy to notice in this connection is that I did not confront the patient with the entire interpretation at once but built up to it piece by piece, a little at a time. I determined how much to interpret by how much the patient seemed ready to hear.

Question: How was the question of when to interpret answered?

Answer: The answer to this question is implicit in the preceding discussions; that is, I communicated further depth-psychological information when the patient appeared to be ready to receive and understand it.

Question: What was the most important strategy regarding how to interpret?

Answer: Perhaps the most important strategy in this regard was to communicate depth-psychological information tentatively rather than authoritatively. In the present illustrative case, for example, I led the patient to further insight gently rather than push her to it.

RECAPITULATION

The technique of clinical interpretation consists, first, of verbal reformulation, and then communication of interpretive understanding to patients in depth-psychological treatments. The communication of interpretive understanding is not necessarily, or even usually, conveyed through formal interpretive statements to the patient, however. The patient gains such insights in various ways, some through the therapist's understanding, others through self-understanding (see Chapter 7), or in subtle subliminal ways that we do not yet fully understand.

Although Freud advocated abstinence, he indicated that by this he did not mean that one should deprive the patient of everything, which no sick person could tolerate.

Some noteworthy changes in therapeutic technique since Freud (by some but not all therapists) include: greater attention to countertransference phenomena; more emphasis on here-and-now relational interactions in the therapeutic relationship; less belief in the therapist's objectivity and authority; viewing depth-psychological therapies as two-person psychologies, with deemphasis on intrapsychic phenomena; more self-disclosure by the therapist of his own inner mental life in the therapeutic process; and the dialectical constructivist attempt to find an optimal position between formal (clinical) authority and personal responsivity and self-expression.

The communication of interpretations is discussed and illustrated in terms of the following major categories: (1) verbal reformulation of interpretive hypotheses, (2) whether (and why) to communicate interpretations, (3) what (and how much) to communicate, (4) when to communicate, and (5) how to communicate interpretations. A clinical case report illustrates these categories and strategies of communicating interpretations.

REFERENCES

Etchegoyen, R. (1989). *The fundamentals of psychoanalytic technique*. London: Karnac Books.

Fenichel, O. (1945). *The psychoanalytic theory of neurosis*. New York: Norton.

French, T. (1958). The art and science of psychoanalysis. *Journal of the American Psychoanalytic Association, 6*, 197–214.

French, T. (1963). The art and science of psychoanalysis. In L. Paul (Ed.), *Psychoanalytic clinical interpretation*. London: Free Press of Glencoe (Macmillan).

Freud, A. (1954). The widening scope of indications for psychoanalysis. *Journal of the American Psychoanalytic Association, 2*, 607–620.

Freud, S. (1910). The future prospects of psycho-analytic therapy. *Standard edition* (Vol. 11, pp. 139–152).

Freud, S. (1915a). Observations on transference love (Further recommendations on the technique of psychoanalysis III). *Standard edition* (Vol. 12, pp. 157–171). London: Hogarth, 1958, p. 165.

Freud, S. (1915b). Remembering, repeating, and working through (Further recommendations on the technique of psycho-analysis II). *Standard edition* (Vol. 12, pp. 145–156). London: Hogarth, 1958.

Freud, S. (1915c). The unconscious. *Standard edition* (Vol. 14, pp. 159–216). London: Hogarth, 1957, pp. 175–176.

Freud, S. (1916–1917). Introductory lectures on psychoanalysis, part 3. *Standard edition* (Vol. 15, pp. 243–296). London: Hogarth, 1963, p. 17.

Greenberg, J. (2001). The analyst's participation: A new look. *Journal of the American Psychoanalytic Association, 49,* 359–380.

Greenberg, J., & Mitchell, S. (1983). *Object relations in psychoanalytic theory.* Cambridge, MA: Harvard Univeristy Press.

Hoffman, I. (1998). *Ritual and spontaneity in the psychoanalytic process.* Hillsdale, NJ: Analytic Press.

Hoffman, I. (1994). Dialectical thinking and the therapeutic action in the psychoanalytic process. *Psychoanalytic Quarterly, 63,* 187–218.

Jacobs, T. (1991). *The use of the self: Countertransference and communication in the analytic situation.* Madison, CT: International Universities Press.

Jacobs, T. (1999). On the question of self-disclosure: Error or advance in technique. *Psychoanalytic Quarterly, 68,* 159–183.

Jones, E. (1938). The significance of the grandfather for the fate of the individual. In *Papers on psychoanalysis* (4th ed., pp. 519–524). Baltimore: Williams, Wood.

Kernberg, O. (1988). Psychic structure and structural change: An ego–psychological–object relational theory viewpoint. *Journal of the American Psychoanalytic Association, 36*(Suppl.), 315–337.

Kernberg, O. (2001). Recent developments in the technical approaches of English-language psychoanalytic schools. *Psychoanalytic Quarterly, 70,* 519–548.

Lacan, J. (1968). *The language of the self: The function of language in psychoanalysis.* Baltimore: Johns Hopkins University Press.

Loewenstein, R. (1958). Remarks on some variations in psychoanalytic technique. *International Journal of Psychoanalysis, 30,* 202–210.

Meissner, W. (2000). The self as relational in psychoanalysis. I. Relational aspects of the self. *Psychoanalysis and Contemporary Thought, 23,* 177–204.

Mitchell, S. (1988). *Relational concepts in psychoanalysis: An integration.* Cambridge, MA: Harvard University Press.

Mitchell, S. (1997). *Influence and autonomy in psychoanalysis.* Hillsdale, NJ: Analytic Press.

Rubovits-Seitz, P. (1998). *Depth-psychological understanding: The methodologic grounding of clinical interpretations.* Hillsdale, NJ: Analytic Press.

Chapter 7

Development of
Self-Interpretive Competence

Question: What is meant by self-interpretive competence, and what is its relevance to the therapeutic process and its outcome?

Answer: Most depth-psychological clinicians appear to agree that an important outcome of a successful analysis or dynamic psychotherapy is the development of self-interpretive (or self-analytic) competence. In the course of their treatments, patients gradually learn how to apply clinical interpretive methods to their own associations, dreams, fantasies, slips of speech, and other interpretable data. As the therapeutic process progresses, gentle but steady encouragement by the therapist appears to reinforce the patient's motivation toward self-mastery, which facilitates a learning process in which more and more of the therapist's specialized interpretive competence is acquired and used with increasing confidence and effectiveness by the patient. The more such competence the patient develops, the more he or she will be able to use it effectively to deal with emotional problems that may occur posttherapeutically.

Question: How can a therapist know whether such competence is developing in the course of the therapeutic process?

Answer: One can observe the patient's coding and recoding of such information as the therapeutic process unfolds over time. During early phases of the treatment, for example, the patient is relatively unfamiliar with the conventions (or "code") of clinical interpretation; but as the therapeutic dialogue progresses, the patient gradually learns some of the key interpretive conventions of depth psychology and becomes increasingly able to anticipate the therapist's interpretations and to apply the conventions to his or her own associations.

Question: What is the history of this concept in the depth psychologies?

Answer: Freud's (1986) own self-analysis was the model for the concept of self-analysis, which he then recommended in the training analyses of psychoanalysts. Much later, Freud (1937) concluded that infantile conflicts have an unusual tenacity, cannot be resolved completely, and thus may be revived again following treatment. These considerations led him to speak of analysis as interminable and to propose that analysts might need to be reanalyzed at intervals—a possible alternative being a continuing self-analysis.

Q**uestion:**   Did these views then come to be applied to patients generally rather than just to psychoanalytic trainees?

A**nswer:**   Yes. These views concerning the importance of self-analysis in training analyses gradually came to be applied by a number of psychoanalysts not only to candidates in psychoanalytic training but to patients generally. One of the earliest and most influential of these writings was by Maria Kramer (1959). In her pioneering study she reported a self-analytic process in herself that she described as occurring spontaneously, extending over a period of months, and resulting in the resolution of persistent problems that had not been resolved during her training analysis or in previous deliberate attempts at self-analysis. On the basis of her self-observations, she postulated the existence of an autonomous self-analytic ego function that she called the autoanalytic function.

Q**uestion:**   Were Kramer's observations supported by other writers?

A**nswer:**   Yes. Helen Beiser (1984) presented another example of self-analysis and reviewed the literature on this subject. At about the same time as Beiser's report, Schlessinger and Robbins (1983, pp. 9–10) published their volume on follow-up studies of patients who had completed successful analyses. They concluded, as Freud had observed, that

> psychic conflicts were not eliminated in the analytic process. The clinical material of the follow-ups demonstrated a repetitive pattern of conflicts. Accretions of insight were evident but

the more significant outcome of the analysis appeared to be the development of a preconsciously active self-analytic function, in identification with the analyzing function of the analyst, as a learned mode of coping with conflicts. As elements of the transference neurosis reappeared and were re-solved, the components of a self-analytic function were demonstrated in self-observation, reality processing, and the tolerance and mastery of frustration, anxiety, and depression. The[se] resources gained in the analytic process persisted, and their vitality was evident in response to renewed stress.

Question: Is self-interpretive competence related to the process of self-observation?

Answer: Yes. Self-observation is one of the basic components of self-interpretation. The most relevant feature of the reflective self-observing process, according to Myerson (1965) and also Hatcher (1973), is its degree of intrapsychic focus—an increasing appreciation of the self's contributions to experience so that the locus of explanation shifts from the outside to the inside (see below, the development of self-interpretive competence in this author's patient, John).

Question: What are the conventions (or "code") of clinical interpretation that patients learn during their therapies?

Answer: Clinicians differ in their answers to this question, but most appear to agree that there is no strict "code." Rather, as Freud (1923) insisted, clinical interpretation is not based on rules but leaves much to the sensitivity, imagination, and judgment of the individual clinician. Thus, interpretive activities are not subject to any hard and fast logical or methodological rules.

Question: Does this mean that clinical interpretations lack any grounding at all?

Answer: No. The grounding of clinical interpretations consists of:

1. A relatively small number of basic, general concepts (or background assumptions) of psychoanalysis and dynamic psychotherapy, namely, the concepts of an unconscious mind, continuity, meaning, determinism, overdetermination, instinctual drives, conflict, defense, repetition, transference, and the importance of childhood experiences;
2. A relatively large number of frequently useful psychodynamic interpretive heuristics—the latter being loosely systematic methodologic procedures that give good results on the whole but do not guarantee them in any particular instance;
3. A grounding of the interpretive process that includes the shifting, ever unfolding context of previously interpreted events, the necessary and progressive modifications of which contribute to the uncertainty and fallibility of clinical interpretations.

Question: How do the basic concepts (or background assumptions) function in the interpretive process, and why are they important?

Answer: What these core concepts of the depth psychologies have most in common is their generality, as a result of which they do not give rise to single but to alternative interpretive hypotheses. Broad, general background assumptions and concepts of this kind do not force interpretations into preconceived conclusions; new, unique interpretations of the data are possible within the general theoretical framework of a science. By contrast, specific clinical theories tend to generate single rather than alternative interpretive hypotheses. Thus, theory-driven clinical interpretations based on specific clinical theories are often not applicable to the individual patient and may interfere with the discovery or construction of unique personal meanings and determinants.

Question: What is a clinical example of developing self-interpretive competence?

Answer:

CASE REPORT:

John was a 30-year-old single man, the youngest of three sons in a wealthy southern family. He came for treatment because of inferiority feelings, occupational instability, and lack of a love life. His eldest brother was the "fair-haired boy" of the family, successful, married, and had children. The second son had been less successful and was killed in an auto accident ten years previously. John was overprotected by his mother, partly because he had been born with

114

several congenital defects, most of which were corrected surgically during his childhood. His father was gruff toward John and took less interest in him than in his older brother. As a result, John had turned all the more to his mother for acceptance and affection. His father complained frequently that his mother was making a "sissy" of him.

In his teens he made a serious suicide attempt and was hospitalized for about a year. His conscious reason for attempting suicide was fear of facing his father about getting caught and expelled from school for forging his father's signature on an excuse from gym classes. In the course of our therapeutic work, however, we found that his unconscious reason for the suicide attempt was intense attraction toward a handsome boy in his gym class. He felt that his father's direst prediction about him—that he would end up homosexual—had come true.

From the time of his suicide attempt at age 17 until his treatment with me at the age of 30, John had been in therapy almost continuously. Presumably because of his intellectual and other limitations, the therapies had been primarily supportive rather than exploratory. When I first saw him and heard the history of his life, I too assumed that his treatment would have to be considerably less than psychodynamic or analytic. His somewhat awkward, unsophisticated, adolescent manner, in addition to his difficulties with language and even pronunciation made it fairly easy to underestimate him. It was only after he had been in treatment with me for about six months that I began to sense more potential in him for a depth-psychological approach. Therefore, after six months of therapy I explained free association to him and asked whether he would like to try it. He said that he would, so his appointments were increased and from that point on his sessions consisted of free association, study of his dreams, and depth-psychological interpretive inquiry.

He had little difficulty in adjusting to the changes in his treatment. My talking much less than before occasioned reactions and comments from him, but actual disturbance about the changes was minimal. He seemed at home with free association—if anything, more relaxed and spontaneous than when we had talked more conversationally.

Early in the second year of this analytic therapy, John was awarded a prize for stimulating the most new business in his company. The following dreams and their interpretation became a turning point in his treatment:

Dreams: A woman at work wanted to kiss me but I was afraid the boss would see us so I told her not to kiss me when he was around. In another dream I was angry at the pope for backing Iran.

Associations: He recalled his father telling his mother that she was making a sissy of John by petting and pampering him and keeping him around the house so much. During his teens he once kissed his mother very passionately, which startled her. Afterward he was afraid she might tell his father. Associations to the pope backing Iran elicited anger at his father for not rescuing him from his mother, by whom he felt he had been "held hostage."

Interpretation: I commented interpretively that in the first dream he blamed his mother for holding on to him, and in the second dream he blamed his father for not rescuing him from his mother. Perhaps he blames *them* to avoid feeling blame himself. He responded sheepishly that he had to admit that the kiss was his own idea and that he probably

116

could have gotten away from his mother if he had really wanted to. But the truth is that he liked being with her.

Note that *I* did the interpreting of these particular dreams and their associations. Note also that my interpretation drew on the basic concept of defense—that he blamed his parents to avoid painful feelings of self-blame. From later developments in his treatment it appeared that he understood both the interpretation and the basic concept underlying it, and as a result was able to apply them to at least some of his subsequent free associations and dreams with a minimum of interpretive guidance from me.

From this point on in his treatment, John took increasing responsibility for his own problems, behavior, and also his treatment. Following the preceding episode, he began to associate more freely, became more adept at observing his own associations, and took increasing interest in attempting to interpret his own productions. During the next several months, for example, an important defense against his competitive feelings and fantasies became evident to both of us and he was as quick to recognize the pattern as I. The pattern was a need to fail—what Freud (1916, pp. 316–331) called the character pathology of being "wrecked by success." For example, soon after receiving the award for new business he very nearly got himself fired for failure to attend required meetings at his company. He connected that behavior with another manifestation of the self-defeating tendency, namely, job hopping—never staying with a job long enough to compete for advancement. He also coupled that insight with a childhood pattern: having been a sick child, he found he could obtain considerable attention from his family by appearing unable to compete. A year later in his treatment he added the still further insight that by being sickly he could often have his mother to himself.

During the third year of John's analysis he showed even more self-interpretive capacity in a "good therapeutic hour," illustrated by a series of dreams and their associations, which included a number of self-interpretations. In recent sessions he had been preoccupied with his father coming to town to discuss family business. During the previous year he had convinced his father to let him handle the investment of some family funds. In an effort to outdo his father by achieving greater returns on the investments, he had speculated in the market and lost money. Knowing that his mishandling of the funds would be reviewed during the coming visit, he anticipated his father's arrival with dread.

In this context of events he started a session by asking, "Did you know that the bridge near here is called Suicide Bridge?" Recently he had experienced a return of his old height phobia, which started in his teens, went away while he was in the hospital at age 17, but returned after he left the hospital and went to visit an older woman whom he had met at the hospital. She lived in a high-rise building, and while looking down from her apartment his height phobia recurred. Coming over the high bridge near my home on the way to his appointment he felt the height phobia again.

He wondered why he had the height phobia. As a boy he liked to climb trees. A son of the family who bought their home hanged himself in the tree John used to climb. Asked about his reaction to that, he replied, "He succeeded, dammit!" (You wish you had?) "Sometimes, because then I wouldn't have to face problems." (What problems at present?) "I'm not sure—maybe facing my father about the money I lost in the market. I haven't told him about it, but it will come up in our discussions next week." (This is beginning to sound like what happened just before your suicide attempt.) He responded with surprise, "Right! I was afraid to face him then, too, for fear he'd be furious. That reminds me of a bunch of dreams I had last night." What appeared to remind him of the dreams was the association about fearing his father— compare the manifest content of the first dream. The connection he made here illustrates his growing ability to think and reason associatively:

> *Dream 1*: I was trying to hide from someone I was afraid of. I became a statue in a fountain, but turtles kept nipping at my pants legs.

> *Dream 2*: David Stockman, who is in charge of the budget office, attempted suicide by swallowing a bunch of pins.

> *Dream 3*: I was living with an older woman whose husband was dead. I think it was the older woman in the hospital whose apartment I visited.

> *Dream 4*: There was a statue covered with ice. I was chipping the ice away. The ice was falling off in big chunks.

He began associating to the dreams spontaneously:

> *Associations to dream 1*: There was a fountain at the mental hospital with a statue in the middle of it. I wasn't just pretending to be a statue—I *was* a statue. Turtles live a long time and have a thick shell—both like my father! That dream sounds like I was trying to hide from my father, but he catches me anyway. (His associations to and interpretations of the turtles demonstrate that he had learned the important role of analogical similarity in the interpretation of symbols.)

> *Interpretation of dream 1*: "A statue sometimes represents a dead person. You tried to escape from guilt toward and fear of your father by death. Have you been thinking of doing that again because of guilt and fear about the investments?" "Yes!" he blurted out. "It has crossed my mind. But I wouldn't actually do it now—at least, I don't think I would . . . but, uh—"

Associations to dream 2: "On the other hand, that second dream about David Stockman swallowing the pins could be me! My mother says I look like him—but she prefers Ronald Reagan." (What about the pins?) "Pins remind me of a man's sperm. They look like sperm cells." He then recalled an earlier dream of swallowing semen, which occurred when his father was visiting and slept in the same room with him. "But how could swallowing my father's sperm be suicidal?" (Here we see an example of his using reflection in search of a possible analogy. His reflection led to recalling that what he feared most when he attempted suicide in his teens was not his father's reaction to forging an excuse from gym classes, but what he knew his father's attitude would be toward John's attraction to a handsome boy in his class. Note how well he is free associating at this point, observing his own associations and attempting to interpret them.)

Interpretation of dream 2: (Perhaps swallowing your father's sperm could be a way of killing off your manhood to keep from competing with him.) "Competing with him about the investments? About mother? I wonder if the investments, my father's money, represents mother to me." (Yet another example of John seeing a cogent analogy.) "I tried everything to get control of the money and then tried to outdo my father with it!" (You also "took some liberties" with it?) "Yeah, I did, didn't I? I took some liberties with Mother, too—like giving her those long passionate kisses during my teens. I was afraid for Father to know about that, too!" (Here one can see that he had learned the important interpretive heuristic that the central character in one's dreams and associations is often oneself. Further associations about the pins reminding him of sperm cells because of their shape again reveals his growing ability to look not only for analogical similarities but also for similarities—relations and patterns—of all kinds in his attempts to interpret his dreams and associations.)

Associations to dream 3: "That reminds me of the next dream about living with the older woman whose husband had died." He then added further relevant associations to that dream and the woman (mother figure) in it: "I happen to know that she tried to make a substitute husband of her son. Maybe she would have done that with me, too"—at which point an insight dawned on him suddenly. He said, "Oh! No wonder the height phobia returned then." (To reinforce his self-interpreted insight, I agreed with the dynamic parallel that he was suggesting and added that, as with his mother, he may have felt that he was getting in over his head with her.) He responded, "For sure! Like the time I kissed Mother so long and it made her all flustered. I was *scared to death* that she'd tell Father and they'd both punish me for it." (Note the allusion of the italicized phrase to the theme of suicide [death], illustrating again how revealing his associations had become.)

Associations to dream 4: "Chipping the ice off the statue seems like what I do in treatment. I chip away at the coatings that cover up my feelings and find out what's underneath. Lately I seem to be chipping away pretty fast and deep. In the dream what lies under the ice is someone dead—*me*! Hmm. I'm getting the feeling that my old suicidal thoughts must have been stronger and lasted longer than I realized!" (Right, and why do you think that is?) He was quiet for a minute, then said, "Guilt! Guilt about wanting to get rid of my Dad, guilt about wanting to get his money, guilt about wanting to outdo him with Mother, guilt about wanting Mother all to myself, and guilt about wanting sex with her. So guilty I should be given the death sentence!"

Question: What was the principal current (thematic) conflict of this session?

Answer: Oedipal rivalry with his father versus guilt and fear of his father's wrath.

Question: What was the precipitant of that conflict?

Answer: The conflict appeared to have been precipitated by his father's coming visit, during which John's mishandling of some family funds was certain to be discussed.

Question: What were the principal defenses against that conflict?

Answer: The principal defense mechanisms against (and attempted solution) of the thematic conflict appeared to be:

Avoidance mechanisms

1. Hiding the truth from his father
2. Symptoms: height phobia, suicidal thoughts

Displacement, substitution, projection, and reaction formation

1. From outdoing his father with his mother to outdoing him with money

2. From his mother to an older woman whose apartment he visited

3. From his own suicidal urges to memories of the boy who actually hanged himself, and to "Suicide Bridge," from which other people had jumped to their deaths

4. Latent homosexual phantasies toward his father

Masochistic, self-punitive mechanisms

1. Motivated failures
2. Denying himself a love life
3. Turning aggression against himself (attempted suicide and suicidal thoughts)

Attempted solution: Attempting to understand and resolve the suicidal thoughts via depth-psychological treatment

Question: What verbal reformulation was employed in my communication to the patient?

Answer: Relatively little verbal reformulation of the previously described session was necessary because the session flowed associatively and dynamically, from beginning to end, with such clarity and spontaneity that both John and I seemed to experience a sense of inevitability about its momentum and meaning. Our collaboration in the therapeutic dialogue was unusually effective and satisfying. For all of these reasons I believe the session represented a "good analytic hour," which Kris (1956) described this way: The "good hour" occurs in patients who are well advanced in therapy:

It may come gradually into its own, say after the first ten or fifteen minutes, when some recent experience has been recounted, which may or may not refer to yesterday's session. Then a dream may come, and associations, and all begins to make sense. In particularly fortunate instances a memory from the near or distant past may present itself with varying degrees of affective charge . . . When the analyst interprets, sometimes all he needs to say can be put into a question. The patient may well do the summing up by himself, and himself arrive at conclusions. Such hours seem as if prepared in advance.

Peterfreund (1983, pp. 67–68) evaluated the significance of "good hours" in the following way:

The good hour is one wherein patient, therapist, as well as competent observers would agree that something important happened, something "true," "real," or meaningful, both cognitively and affectively. Often, these are dramatic hours, but they need not be. Good hours are especially important because so many of our sessions are murky, uncertain, confused, and it is often difficult to know what has happened. The good hour is akin to a successful experiment which has given clear-cut, valid, unambiguous results.

I believe the session described was a "good hour." Sessions of that kind were not rare in John's treatment but occurred several times a year during the latter half of his therapy. Near the end of John's treatment he met, fell in love with, and married a woman with whom he seemed very compatible. They had two children who appeared to be developing well.

In follow-up sessions with John after his treatment was completed he free associated well, observed his own associations, and continued to show considerable ability to interpret and understand latent meanings and determinants in his own associations, dreams, and so forth—all of which suggest that the gains in self-interpretive competence acquired during his treatment had been retained and were continuing posttherapeutically.

Question: Is the development of self-interpretive competence related to interpretive technique during treatment?

Answer: Yes. Contrary to Theodore Reik's (Kris, 1949, p. 267) advice to present interpretations in the form of statements without adding one's reasons for their formulation, and Etchegoyen's (1989, p. 374) insistence that in order to avoid "the mortal sin of intellectualization . . . the analyst must be like Cassandra the slave, offering her prophesies without ever explaining them," I believe that it may be advantageous in promoting the development of self-interpretive competence if the therapist provides some relevant information about how his or her interpretations are construed, for example: calling attention to key clues in the clinical material that appeared to suggest possible latent content; explaining specific psychodynamic heuristics that may have suggested a particular latent meaning or determinant; mentioning how alternative constructions have been considered and assessed in selecting the most plausible interpretation; and other such basic methods and concepts of one's interpretive approach.

Question: Does this mean that the therapist "teaches" the patient how to interpret his own material during treatment?

Answer: No. I do not mean that the therapist should attempt to "teach" the patient how to interpret clinical data, at least not didactically, and I do not mean to imply that the origins of self-interpretive competence consist solely of what patients learn about this process in the course of their treatment. What I have in mind is that, conceivably, the more the therapist shares his or her interpretive reasoning and strategies with the patient, the more opportunity the patient may have to develop clinical interpretive competence. Also, it seems likely that giving the patient ample opportunity to use and to practice his or her own self-interpretive capacity during the therapeutic process may promote more robust development of self-interpretive competence. I also suggest that such a practice might be useful at times in all depth-psychological treatments.

Question: Do the therapist's interventions act primarily as suggestions regarding the "code" of clinical interpretation?

Answer: Probably not. If clinical interpretations were presented as authoritative statements they might well have a significant suggestive effect, but if they are conveyed tentatively and collaboratively as possibilities the likelihood of suggestive influence is reduced. Another important interpretive convention that the patient needs to learn, both for effective collaboration in the therapeutic relationship and for future self-inquiry, is that depth-psychological interpretation is difficult and fallible, which calls for an undogmatic, scientifically skeptical attitude on the part of the interpreter toward his or her own interpretations. Ideally, therefore, the patient learns our interpretive conventions not under the pressure of suggestions from, or an inner need to please, the therapist, but from repeated experiences of mutual search for the most plausible interpretation at a given time. If suggestive effects appear to occur in connection with interventions, those effects themselves then become a necessary focus of interpretive inquiry.

RECAPITULATION

During the course of a well-going therapeutic process patients become increasingly able to interpret their own productions. A learning process appears to occur in both the patient and the therapist, that is, the therapist becomes increasingly familiar with the patient's recurring patterns of conflicts and defenses, and the patient becomes increasingly confident and effective in associating freely, observing his or her own productions, and learning to apply the conventions or "code" of depth-psychological interpretation to his or her own associations and other data.

The principal prerequisite knowledge or conventions of our interpretive approach appear to include:

1. A relatively small number of basic general (core) concepts or background assumptions of psychoanalysis and dynamic psychotherapy, in contrast to specific clinical theories— the general concepts comprising an unconscious mind, meaning, continuity, determinism, overdetermination, instinctual drives, conflict, defense, repetition, transference, and the importance of childhood experiences;
2. A relatively large number of often useful psychodynamic heuristics;
3. The previous, progressively modified interpretations employed in the entire therapeutic process;
4. A realization and acceptance that clinical interpretation is difficult and fallible, which calls for a skeptical, scientifically tentative attitude toward one's interpretations.

The technique of interpretation contributes to the development of self-interpretive competence by the therapist's gentle but steady encouragement for the patient to try to understand his or her own productions, and by sharing with the patient relevant clues in the clinical data and clinical interpretive conventions that contributed to the therapist's own understanding.

REFERENCES

Beiser, H. (1984). Example of self-analysis. *Journal of the American Psychoanalytic Association, 32,* 3–12.

Etchegoyen, R. (1989). *The fundamentals of psychoanalytic technique.* London: Karnac Books.

Freud, S. (1923). Two encyclopaedia articles. *Standard edition* (Vol. 18, pp. 235–262). London: Hogarth, 1955, p. 239.

———. (1937). Analysis terminable and interminable. *Standard edition* (Vol. 23, 209–254). London: Hogarth, 1964.

———. (1986). *Freud's self-analysis* (P. Graham, Trans.). London: Hogarth. (Original work published).

Hatcher, R. (1973). Insight and self-observation. *Journal of the American Psychoanalytic Association, 21,* 377–398.

Kramer, M. (1959). On the continuation of the analytic process after psychoanalysis (A self-observation). *International Journal of Psychoanalysis, 40,* 17–25.

Kris, E. (1949). *The inner experience of a psychoanalyst.* London: Allen & Unwin.

Kris, E. (1956). On some vicissitudes of insight in psychoanalysis. *International Journal of Psychoanalysis, 37,* 445–455. Also in (1975), *Selected papers of Ernst Kris,* pp. 252–271. New Haven, CT: Yale University Press.

Kris, E. (1983). *The process of psychoanalytic therapy.* Hillsdale, NJ: Analytic Press.

Myerson, P. (1965). Modes of insight. *Journal of the American Psychoanalytic Association, 13,* 771–792.

Peterfreund, E. (1983). *The Process of Psychoanalytic Therapy.* Hillsdale, NJ: The Analytic Press.

Schlessinger, N., & Robbins, F. (1983). *A developmental view of the psychoanalytic process: Follow-up studies and their consequences.* New York: International Universities Press.

II

Some Postclassical Approaches

to Clinical Interpretation

Chapter 8

Kohut's Self-Psychological Approach

Question: What characterizes Kohut's approach to clinical interpretation?

Answer: Two main things: (1) his insistence that empathy is the principal method of achieving understanding of latent mental processes (or in some of his writings [Kohut, 1984], the only one); and (2) his extensive use of self-psychological clinical theory (which he developed) in formulating interpretive hypotheses.

Question: Is empathy involved in how the therapist listens?

Answer: Yes. "Kohut argued that Freud's recommendations for evenly suspended attention require more than a mere negative suspension of conscious, goal-directed, logical thought processes.

They also require the positive use of the analyst's prelogical modes of perceiving and thinking" (Wolf, 1984, p. 150). "Evenly hovering attention, in other words, is the analyst's active empathic response to the analysand's free associations" (Kohut, 1971).

Question: What does empathy consist of operationally?

Answer: At the same time that the therapist listens to the patient, he or she attempts to *sense* and *imagine* what the patient is experiencing (Wolf, 1984, p. 150). Kohut (1972–1976, p. 228) described his use of the empathic method in clinical interpretation this way: we think ourselves into another person by various cues that we get from him. The cues include the traditional search for precipitating factors and events. In addition, self psychologists are especially alert to clues of "empathic disruptions" (see below). On the basis of these cues, the therapist then reconstructs the patient's inner life as if he were that other person. In other words, the therapist trusts the resonance of the essential likeness between himself and the patient.

Question: How does empathy contribute to the formulation (as opposed to the construal) of interpretations?

Answer: Empathy "guides" the therapist to the patient's introspective experience. Self-psychological theory then leads the therapist to form tentative hypotheses about the conscious and unconscious meanings of those experiences (Wolf, 1984, pp. 150–157).

Question: Did Freud recognize the role of empathy in understanding latent mental processes?

Answer: Yes. He stated that empathy makes possible "any attitude at all towards another mental life" (Freud, 1905) and that empathy "plays the largest part in our understanding of what is inherently foreign to our ego in other people" (Freud, 1921).

Question: Did Kohut consider his view of empathy and its role in depth-psychological treatments to differ from Freud's?

Answer: No. He felt that empathy is the basis of all depth psychology; he stated clearly that the self psychologist's empathy is not essentially different than that of the traditional psychoanalyst and that self psychology does not achieve cure by a novel kind of empathy (Goldberg, 1998, p. 243).

Question: What is meant by *empathic resonance* and *empathic immersion*?

Answer: Empathic resonance is what self-psychological therapists attempt to achieve by close attunement to what the patient is experiencing. Empathic immersion refers to the process of a prolonged, sustained state of empathy with a patient in an attempt to understand his or her inner experiences.

Question: Did Kohut acknowledge that the use of empathy in that way could yield errors in interpretation?

Answer: Yes. He noted that "even with like experiences [between patient and therapist] there are many possible errors." Also in this connection, he wrote that "we must have the capacity to postpone closures and to apply closures tentatively, observing the [patient's] reactions to our tentative interpretations, and to consider as many explanations as possible" (Kohut, 1984, p. 172).

Question: How did he employ empathy in search of alternative interpretive hypotheses?

Answer: By use of what he called "trial empathy," to "consider the greatest possible number of explanatory configurations. The more the better" (Kohut, 1984, p. 184). He added that the skill of the intuitive psychoanalytic observer is to avoid falling automatically into the conviction of "that's it," for "the sense that you have all the evidence to sustain one conclusion should not close your mind to searching for other conclusions. You should keep in mind that despite the seeming cohesion and fit, it might yet be something else" (Kohut, 1984, p. 184).

Question: Did Kohut feel that empathy could be overdone in depth-psychological treatments?

Answer: Yes. He wrote: "If empathy, instead of limiting its role to that of a data-collecting process, begins to replace the explanatory phase of psychoanalysis . . . then we are witnessing a deterioration of scientific standards [and their replactment by] a sentimentalizing to subjectivity" (Kohut, 1971, pp. 300–301).

Question: What is meant by "disruptions of empathy," and how do self psychologists conceptualize their importance in the therapeutic process?

Answer: Ernest Wolf (1984, pp. 153–154) writes:

> From the patient's point of view, i.e., from the point of view of the patient's *experience*, it is a feeling of not having been listened to or of having been misunderstood or criticized, or some other repetition of what it felt like as a child when, inevitably, the parent could not be perfectly attuned to the child. It is a genuine experience for the patient—it is real, not a distortion. At that moment the [therapist], in fact, does not understand something. This something may be extremely trivial to the [therapist], who is likely to have sensitivities different from the patient's. But it is not trivial to the patient . . . A possible interpretation to the patient that his perception of reality was distorted would [only add] insult to injury. A proper interpretation, rather, acknowledges the patient's reality and tries to explain its meaning to him . . . Disruptions are brought to an end by interpretation and explanation."

By these means the relationship with the therapist is repaired and the patient's psychic integrity is restored. Self psychologists believe that such disruptions, and their repair, are the crux of the therapeutic process and of cure.

Question: What is a clinical example of an empathic disruption and its repair?

Answer: Ernest Wolf (1984, pp. 145–146), an early follower of Kohut, describes the following clinical experience:

CASE REPORT:

During a period in the treatment when the patient had initiated some appointment changes, he talked at length about the struggle in his office to get rid of an unsatisfactory employee. Then he commented on how much more convenient the new appoinment schedule was for him. While listening to these associations, Wolf picked up his appointment book and made a brief notation. Evidently the patient heard something, possibly the therapist's motion or the sound of his pen writing. The patient fell silent; after a while Wolf suggested that his writing had disturbed the patient. The patient said he was not sure, although he agreed that he was aware of a noise and felt annoyed.

The next day the patient reported a surge of angry feelings after leaving the therapist's office. It made him furious that the therapist was writing in his appointment book and not really listening to him. He felt ignored and helpless to do anything about it. Even though he told himself what the therapist had done was relatively minor, he could not control his mounting tension and slept poorly that night. In the morning he recalled a fragment of a dream: He was at the house of a friend with whom he was having an animated conversation when the friend's wife came in and both of them walked into another room. The patient and therapist agreed about the dream that, as in his previous session, he felt ignored and left out. Further associations led to memories of his parents being so caught up in their own interests that he felt shunted aside, ignored, neglected. He could see at this point that he had reexperienced with the therapist a set of feelings that were originally part of a repeated pattern of childhood events, and began to realize his genuine need for a different kind of response from his parents in the past, and from the therapist in the present. An appropriate interpretation accepts that, as a child, the patient could hardly have felt differently under the circumstances and that the current experience in the therapeutic relationship inevitably had the same meaning to him.

Question: How did Kohut conceptualize the process by which such events in the treatment lead to cure?

Answer: Each disruption–restoration cycle increases the trust that one can be understood, and that one can learn to understand others, The increasing trust in the self and others results, clinically, in fewer disruptions, decreasing intensity of affective storms when disruptions do occur, and greater tolerance for being "out of tune" with the therapist. This does not mean, however, that autonomy, self-sufficiency, and independence of others has developed (Wolf, 1984, p. 155). Kohut (1984) described the process of strengthening the self as occurring by replacment of archaic object needs with an empathic resonance with the therapist, a view that has similarities to the concept of "corrective emotional experience" proposed originally by Alexander and French (1946). Sooner or later, according to Kohut, the experience of empathic resonance with the therapist will lead the patient to an increased ability to recognize potential sources of empathic resonance in his daily life.

Question: In what ways is Kohut's approach similar to Freud's?

Answer: In the essay "How Kohut Actually Worked," Miller (1985) reports that "In general, Kohut was a 'Classicist' in the sense that he tended to focus first on the transference relationship and, later, when the material seemed propitious, to link this up with genetic material in an increasingly broad and explanatory manner." He also notes that Kohut practiced an essentially "expectant" form of analysis, that is, he was sparing in his interpretations and preferred to wait for further material to clarify underlying dynamics. As far as technique is concerned, Kohut (1971, pp. 224–225) referred to Freud's technique as an "especially apt example" of the tone that should be employed also in interpreting narcissistic personality structures to patients. He stated emphatically that self psychology relies on the same tools as traditional analysis (interpretation followed by working through in an atmosphere of abstinence). He added that "It is not enough for the analyst to be 'nice' to his patients, to be 'understanding,' 'warmhearted,' 'endowed with the human touch'; for all of the evidence now available indicates that these attributes cure neither the classical neuroses nor the analyzable disturbances of the self" (Kohut, 1984, pp. 75, 95).

Question: Do other self psychologists agree with Kohut about these similarities with the classical approach?

Answer: Many, if not most, do. Goldberg (1978, p. 80) asserts, for example, that "a correct or ideal emotional position on the part of the analyst is insufficient by itself; interpretation must carry the brunt of the analytic process." He pointed out further (Goldberg, 1978, pp. 205–206):

> The analyst does not actively soothe; he interprets the analysand's yearning to be soothed. The analyst does not actively mirror; he interprets the need for confirming responses. The analyst does not actively admire or approve grandiose expectations; he explains their role in the psychic economy. The analyst does not fall into passive silence; he explains why his interventions are felt to be intrusive. Of course, the analyst's mere presence, or the fact that he talks, or, especially, the fact that he understands, all have soothing and self-confirming effects on the patient, *and they are so interpreted.* Thus the analytic ambience that makes work possible becomes itself an object for analytic interpretation. The whole analytic process in this way blocks exploitation for mere gratification.

Question: Is there a good clinical example of the continuities between Kohut's approach and the classical Freudian approach?

Answer: In Miller's (1985, pp. 16–17) essay "How Kohut Actually Worked," a case treated by Miller and supervised by Kohut illustrates how thoroughly Kohut had integrated his self-psychological approach with that of traditional psychoanalysis:

CASE REPORT:

The patient was a highly successful man in his 30's, married with several children, who complained of diffuse, restless anxiety. Miller and Kohut agreed that the diagnosis was narcissistic personality disorder, and that the predominant transference in the analysis was an idealizing one. The clinical material that follows is a paraphrase of an appointment during the last two years of the patient's analysis:

The analyst had cancelled the previous appointment. The patient came in saying he was exhausted and depressed, which he connected (intellectually) with the missed appointment. He described an exciting sexual experience with his wife in which she was on top of him, moving about and masturbating while fully clothed. That night he dreamed that the rear end of their small station wagon burst into flames, which the patient extinguished with a garden hose. Then he was supposed to insert his penis in a certain-shaped can held by a woman. He was reminded of a previous dream in which he was supposed to insert his penis into a disposal. He mentioned being hungry several times and recalled a movie of a young man eating prodigious amounts of food. He said he was hungry enough to eat a horse, which the analyst connected with the missed appointment. Later he said he was hungry enough to eat the picture on the analyst's wall and that he could almost eat the couch. The analyst commented that the patient's eating fantasies were getting closer to him. At that point the patient reported fantasies of sucking ferociously, then more passively, on someone's penis, then someone's breast. He recalled the breast pump his father used to obtain milk from his mother's breast for the patient's hospitalized infant brother. At that point he said he felt less fatigued, more energized.

Kohut noted that the session contained a consistent sequence of "classical material." That is, after missing the appointment, the patient came in with a dream of sexual excitement which was probably homosexual, indicated by the "rear end of the car in flames." Then a reference to castration fear in the associated dream of putting his penis in a disposal. And finally the orality, which could have been toward the analyst's penis or may have involved oral incorporation of the analyst. Kohut suggested that the material could have been interpreted in essentially classical terms: "A classical interpretation of this kind can be made when the material is this clear in the analysis of a narcissistic personality disorder or, for that matter in the analysis of any other type of condition, assuming the other indicators of appropriateness of interpretation are favorable."

Kohut also felt, however, that the most central aspect of this session was the patient's idealizing transference to Miller, in which he reacted to the analyst as the good father he did not have while growing up. The analyst's cancelling the previous appointment and not being available over the weekend constituted a narcissistic injury that produced some fragmentation of the patient's self. By the time he returned for the present appointment, however, the breach had healed. In a complete interpretation, Kohut concluded, one would include the narcissistic injury and the break in the self–selfobject relationship; but, he added, one could also interpret the patient's response to the interruption of the relationship "in an essentially classical manner."

Question: What are the principal differences between Kohut's approach and the classical approach?

Answer: Mainly the theoretical concepts of self psychology, for example, the concept that "empathic failures" by parents are a (if not the) major source of psychopathology, not only in narcissistic personality disorders but in all neuroses. Thus, Kohut's self psychology is referred to by some analysts as a "deficiency theory" of psychopathology, i.e., in the sense that the parents did not provide enough, or the right kind, of attention to the patient as a child to promote healthy development of the child's narcissism and self. As Wolf (1984) observed, after empathy guides the therapist to the patient's introspective experience, theory then leads the therapist to form tentative hypotheses about the meanings of the patient's experiences. The latter step in the self-psychological interpretive process thus involves a form of doctrinal interpretation.

Question: Is present-day self psychology still influenced predominantly by Kohut's views and approach?

Answer: In a recent overview of self psychology since Kohut, Goldberg (1998, p. 240) describes the development of three main branches within self psychology that compete for influence in the field: the traditional, intersubjective, and relational groups. What is most surprising in Goldberg's review is how little emphasis is given to Kohut's concepts even among the traditional group of self psychologists. With respect to the traditional group, Goldberg refers to only two main contributions by Kohut: the concepts of selfobjects and of selfobject transferences. Goldberg concludes that "self psychology is working itself free from an absolute allegiance to Kohut" and that Kohut's original aim for self psychology to have an established place within organized psychoanalysis has given way to the rather surprising emergence embodied in a solid group of clinicans and investigators outside of the psychoanalysis that Kohut knew.

REFERENCES

Alexander, F., & French, T. (1946). *Psychoanalytic therapy: Principles and applications.* New York: Norton.

Freud, S. (1905). Three essays on the theory of sexuality. *Standard edition* (Vol. 7, pp. 130–243). London: Hogarth, 1958, pp. 186, 201, 220.

Freud, S. (1921). Group psychology and the analysis of the ego. *Standard edition* (Vol. 18, pp. 69–143). London: Hogarth, 1955, p. 108.

Goldberg, A. (1998). Self psychology since Kohut. *Psychoanalytic Quarterly, 67,* 240–255.

Goldberg, A. (Ed.). (1978). *The psychology of the self: A casebook.* New York: International Universities Press.

Kohut, H. (1971). *The analysis of the self.* New York: International Universities Press. (Monograph No. 4 of *The psychoanalytic study of the child*).

Kohut, H. (1972–1976). *Heinz Kohut: The Chicago Institute lectures* (P. Tolpin & M. Tolpin, Ed.). Hillsdale, NJ: Analytic Press, 1996.

Kohut, H. (1984). *How does analysis cure?* (P. Stepansky & A. Goldberg, Ed.). Chicago: University of Chicago Press.

Miller, J. (1985). How Kohut actually worked. In A. Goldberg (Ed.), *Progress in self psychology* (Vol. 1, pp. 13–30). New York: Guilford.

Wolf, E. (1984). Disruptions in the psychoanalytic treatment of disorders of the self. In P. Stepansky & A. Goldberg (Eds.), *Kohut's legacy,* pp. 143–156. Hillsdale, NJ: Analytic Press.

Chapter 9

Hoffman's Dialectical Constructivist Approach

Question: What does Hoffman mean by *dialectical constructivism?*

Answer: Ogden (1986) defines dialectic this way:

> A dialectic is a process in which each of two opposing concepts creates, informs, preserves, and negates the other, each standing in a dynamic (ever changing) relationship with the other.

The "dialectic" part of Hoffman's (1994, pp. 194–198) term refers to certain tensions that exist within the depth-psychological therapist, the patient, and the therapeutic process itself—tensions that can be described as struggles between opposing inclinations. The therapist, for example, struggles between his or her formal clinical discipline and authority on the one hand, and an inclination toward personal responsiveness and self-expression on the other. The dialectic counterpart in the patient involves preoccupation with and attachment to the therapist and treatment versus the temptation to exclude them in favor of other interests, narcissistic or object related. The tolerance of these tensions within each participant goes hand in hand with tolerating and nourishing the creative potentials of the tension in the other.

The "constructivism" part of the term refers to the viewpoint that depth-psychological therapies involve the interdependent participation of both patient and therapist, and that the latent meanings and determinants identified in the therapeutic work are not the result of objective observation of the patient by the therapist, but are jointly constructed (improvised on the basis of shared, necessarily speculative interpretations) by both participants.

Question: How does the therapist's dialectical struggle influence the process of clinical interpretation?

Answer: The influence is mainly (though not completely) on interpretive technique, that is, whether, what, when, and how to intervene. Hoffman (1992) writes:

> On the side of analytic discipline, first, however much it is learned and internalized in a process of professional socialization, such an attitude gets into the analyst's bones so that it expresses a very important aspect of him- or herself. Second, that discipline, to begin with, is not simply imposed from outside, but represents a special kind of development of the analyst's potential for attention to the experience of others. And third, although the analyst speaks partly in the context of the role of disciplined expert, his or her *voice* can and should remain personally expressive. The effect of the dialectic is to encourage what Schafer [1974] called "talking to patients," as

opposed to the "impersonal diction" [involved in] following a "pseudoanalytic model." With regard to the other pole in the dialectic, moments of personal self-revelation or spontaneous action on the part of the analyst can be located within, and intuitively guided by, a sense of their place in the process as a whole . . . So, on the one hand, psychoanalytic discipline can be self-expressive and, on the other hand, the analyst's self-expression may reflect a complex, intuitive kind of psychoanalytic discipline.

Question: Is the therapist's dialectical struggle integrated in any way?

Answer: Yes. Despite the tension between the dialectically opposing poles of the struggle, "each tendency is also reflected in a substantial way in the other. Thus, the analyst who behaves 'naturally' would be incorporating in his or or actions the sense of discipline that is intrinsic to his or her sense of identity as an analyst" (Hoffman, 1994, p. 198).

Question: How does Hoffman conceptualize the special sense of analytic restraint that remains indispensable to practice?

Answer: He concludes that there is clinical wisdom in the requirement that the therapist abstain from the kind of personal involvement with patients that might develop into an ordinary social situation, for some acceptance by the patient of the recognizably technical aspect of the therapist's behavior is essential. On the other hand, if the therapist is too abstinent or self-negating, the patient's need for the therapist to survive and benefit from the patient's influence would not be met (Winnicott, 1971). Hoffman (1994, p. 194) writes:

> So, on the one hand, a sense of psychoanalytic discipline, which includes restrictions on the extent and nature of the analyst's involvement provides the backdrop for whatever spontaneous, personal interactions the participants engage in. On the one hand, given our current understanding of how important it is that analysts allow themselves to be affected and known to some significant degree by their patients, the restrictions are more qualified than they once were . . . Now, instead of "throwing away the Book," we place it temporarily in the background while the analyst's distinctive self-expression moves into the foreground. The opposite holds as well. When the analyst's more standard, formal, detached, reflective and interpretive stance is in the foreground, the aspect of the relationship that reflects his or her more personal engagement can still be sensed in the background.

Question: What is a clinical illustration of Hoffman's approach?

Answer:

CASE REPORT:

Hoffman (1994, pp. 201–213) reports the case of a female medical student in her late 20s who insisted on sitting up instead of lying down on the couch. Her father was a

Holocaust survivor who was compulsive and tyrannical about many trivial matters in the home and family. If things were not just so he became enraged. In his rigid and authoritarian behavior he seemed at times to have identified with his Nazi persecutors. At the same time he was an energetic, charismatic figure, successful in business, athletic, and an outdoorsman. In her early years the patient saw him as powerful and exciting, and she worshipped him; but later she became bitterly disappointed and disillusioned in him, regarding him as stingy, self-centered, and unable to show affection. He would never initiate such contact himself. Hoffman and the patient gradually recognized that just coming for her sessions involved a great deal of humiliation and feeling of submission on her part. Lying down while the therapist sat up added too much insult to injury.

Hoffman presents the following episode with the patient to illustrate the way therapeutic action can occur in response to the dialectical interplay between analytic discipline and personal participation, and between formal clinical authority (which operates silently in the background) and an atmosphere of spontaneity and mutuality. In the third year of the patient's analysis, her transference took the form of demands for a kind of maternal preoccupation with her needs, which she felt her mother had reserved for her sickly and vulnerable younger sister. The patient felt she had been so intensely jealous of her sister and hostile toward both her and her mother that she considered herself greedy, ungrateful, and unloveable, and she hated herself for those feelings. The derivative of this in her analysis was that she often felt that she was an impossibly difficult patient and that the therapist wanted to be rid of her.

Following a move to a new apartment, she became obsessed with a noise from a garbage chute adjacent to the apartment. At that time she was an advanced medical student going through very stressful rotations. She became increasingly angry and anxious, and felt that she was reacting to the stresses just the way her father would. One morning during this time she called the therapist and asked for an appointment early in the day rather than her usual afternoon time. The therapist could not arrange the change on such short notice. When she came in at her regular time she announced that she was there for just one reason—to get some Valium to calm her down and help her get some sleep. She knew that Hoffman was a psychologist and could not prescribe for her, but insisted that he must know someone who could help her get some medication. Hoffman tried to maintain a "proper" analytic attitude, pointing out that even if it were true that a tranquilizer would help right then, the idea that she had to get it from him was irrational in view of other resources she had. So the demand that *he* give it to her must represent something else, something very important, but to get her the pill might obscure more than clarify what the need was. She would not accept this interpretation and persisted relentlessly in her demand that the therapist address the issue at face value.

What ensued was that under the pressure of her demand and—perhaps the therapist's intuition—he asked her whether she had an internist whom she could ask for a prescription. She said she did, but was not sure how he would feel about it because it had been a long time since she saw him for a checkup. Hoffman said, "Well, if you give me his number I'll call him right now." She was surprised and delighted, and gave him the number, which he called. While waiting for the doctor to come to the phone the patient began whispering in an animated way, "This is crazy; I could get a friend to do this; I could do this myself." She was smiling but seemed embarrassed. Hoffman identified himself to the doctor and said he thought it would be okay, if the patient called, to give her a tranquilizer. The doctor said it was no problem, and to have her call him. After Hoffman hung up, the patient and therapist began talking, and she was receptive for the first time to exploring the meaning of the whole transaction.

About the episode, Hoffman comments that it clearly mattered to the patient that it was he, the analyst, who did this, a person who occupied a special place in the patient's mental life. The hierarchical and asymmetrical aspects of the arrangement provide the backdrop that give such moments of mutuality, cumulatively, their power to affect deeply entrenched and long-standing patterns of internal and external object relations. Exploration of the episode's meaning continued sporadically over several weeks, and a number of important insights emerged. The patient now recognized that she had been very angry because the therapist could not see her earlier that day. She needed something to legitimize what she recognized as childish— the demand that the therapist see her whenever she wanted him to. That demand was linked to another important issue. During that month she had been coming for appointments only three times a week, ostensibly because of her hectic schedule. Hoffman had agreed to that change very reluctantly and "under protest," with the understanding that they would continue to search for a mutually agreeable fourth appointment time. Now the patient admitted, to Hoffman's surprise, that she felt he had given in "too easily" about the appointment frequency. She thought to herself that he was probably relieved not to have to see her so often and had the fantasy that she was as annoying to the therapist as the garbage chute was to her. But she felt deserted, left alone to cope with her miseries, condensed symbolically with the garbage chute. The whole sequence repeated her experience with her mother, who was all too ready, the patient felt, not to visit her if the patient said she was busy. Shortly after this they resumed meeting four times a week and continued on that basis to the end of the treatment.

Question: To what extent does Hoffman employ countertransference cues in the interpretive process?

Answer: He states (Hoffman, 1994, p. 205) that although he has the conviction that his experience in the therapeutic process reflects directly on his own history and may shed light on something in the patient's, his attention does not necessarily gravitate toward specific details in his childhood that complement or parallel those in the patient's experience. To the extent that his focus is on himself, it stays on his own immediate experience as it relates to the patient's immediate experience and to the patient's history. He argues that attention to the specific historical origins of his countertransference could detract from struggling with the nuances of the immediate clinical experience with the patient, for within a given therapy session the process is continuous and the therapist is called on to listen and respond continuously, without the benefit of a "time-out."

Question: On what are clinical interpretations grounded in Hoffman's approach?

Answer: The short answer is "uncertainty." The long answer tells why: Moore (1999, pp. 105–107) points out that Hoffman's model remains basically an attempt to ground psychoanalysis and clinical interpretation in the uncertainty that is inherent in the continuous joint improvisations of shared, necessarily speculative interpretations of clinical experiences. In the constructivist model, the therapist is as fallible as the patient, whether he realizes it or not. In addition, all clinical data are also joint creations, "marked by uncertainty," and are never simply discoveries. For Hoffman (1987), therefore, the therapist ultimately finds his or her most solid ground specifically in uncertainty:

> The alternative that I am advocating is to have as a working assumption the idea that a patient's desires generally involve a complex, shifting hierarchical arrangement of needs and wishes, and that it is virtually impossible to formulate an assessment of their relative weights and positions in that instant when the participating analyst is called upon to respond. After all, the analyst's actions (whether interpretations or other kinds of responses) are themselves embedded in and even partially constituting of his perpetually fluctuating arrangement of desires. Thinking it over is a response too, of course, which can be plausibly interpreted by the patient in various ways.

Thus it can be said of Hoffman that he looks much less for a solution to not knowing than he seeks a way of consciously conducting depth-psychological therapy within the context of uncertainty. Although his perspective is at its best when he takes a stance of not having an answer, he does conceive of some "ambiguous givens" in the participants' experiences, for example (Hoffman, 1994, p. 111):

> Constructive activity goes on in relation to more or less ambiguous *givens* in the patient's and the analyst's experience.

In fact some of those givens are virtually *indisputable* elements in the experiences of the participants and any plausible interpretation would have to take them into account or at least not contradict them. This goes for interpretations by each of the participants of experiences of the other as well as for interpretations that each directs toward himself or herself. Moreover, even the *ambiguous* aspects are not *amorphous.* They have properties that are amenable to a variety of interpretations, maybe even infinite interpretations, especially if we take into account all the nuances that language and tone make possible. But infinite does not mean unlimited in the sense that anything goes.

As Moore (1999, p. 107) points out, Hoffman's reference to "more or less ambiguous" suggests the possibility of more or less *not* ambiguous, that is, more or less definite and perhaps even more or less verifiable:

Moore adds, "Still, one has to respect the attempt, which is nothing less than an attempt to reconcile a putative abandonment of positivism with common sense for which a kind of culturally accepted positivism has provided the common historical foundation . . . [After all,] Freud built psychoanalysis on . . . a positivist conception of history. No one can ignore that conception without losing a central source of the meaning of psychoanalysis."

REFERENCES

Hoffman, I. (1987). The value of uncertainty in psychoanalytic practice [Discussion of paper by E. Wittenberg]. *Contemporary Psychoanalysis, 334*, 205–215.

Hoffman, I. (1992). Expressive participation and psychoanalytic discipline. *Contemporary Psychoanalysis, 28*, 1–15.

Hoffman, I. (1994). Dialectical thinking and therapeutic action in the psychoanalytic process. *Psychoanalytic Quarterly, 63,* 187–218.

Hoffman, I. (1996). The intimate and ironic authority of the psychoanalytic presence. *Psychoanalytic Quarterly, 665,* 102–136.

Moore, R. (1999). *The creation of reality in psychoanalysis.* Hillsdale NJ: Analytic Press.

Ogden, T. (1986). *The matrix of the mind: The therapist's subjectivity in the therapeutic process.* Northvale, NJ: Aronson.

Schafer, R. (1974). Talking to patients in psychotherapy. *Bulletin of the Menninger Clinic, 38,* 503–515.

Winnicott, D. (1971), *Reality and playing.* New York: Basic Books.

Chapter 10

Schafer's Multifaceted Approach

Question: What is meant by Schafer's multifaceted approach?

Answer: His numerous writings, extending over thirty-five years, have focused at various times on language, action, narration, and hermeneutics. At times he has emphasized one or another of these subjects, but eventually the issues coalesce in his perspective to form a multifaceted view of the therapeutic process and clinical interpretation.

Question: How do the issues of language, action, narration, and hermeneutics coalesce in his approach?

Answer: With respect to hermeneutics, Schafer's overall perspective of depth psychology is that he views psychoanalysis as an interpretive discipline rather than a natural science. As such, it deals with language and equivalents of language, and interpretations are redescriptions or retellings of action along clinical, theoretical lines.

To illustrate the coalescence of language, action, and narration, he identifies (Schafer, 1983, pp. 241–248) many locutions by patients used to disclaim their own actions and notes the defensive and resistant function of disclaiming—denying responsibility by attributing "agency" to entities (including impulses and thoughts) rather than to oneself. Through such disclaiming, the patient pictures himself as the victim or witness of happenings whose origins and explanations lie outside his sphere of influence. By doing so the patient attempts to preclude feeling anxious, guilty, ashamed, or otherwise disturbed by his actions.

When people are disclaiming action they are fantasizing, imagining their minds as existing in a split up or split off way. Schafer views such acts of imagining as narratives that constitute experience rather than as reports of some introspectable experience. Therefore, disclaiming is narrative action; and in each case the narrative composed and the subjective world being constituted may be inferred from the patient's language and context.

Question: What is a clinical example of these concepts?

Answer: A patient says, "I have been crushed by this defeat," which is a metaphorical expression, but in some sense people *are* "crushed" when they say genuinely that that is how they feel. They slump physically, lower their voices, behave in a listless or dazed manner, and exhibit other such signs. Being "crushed" is thus psychically real to them. For this reason the clinical listener must always listen literally, as well as in other ways, to achieve depth-psychological understanding of such expressions.

Question: Does Schafer advocate the use of "action language" exclusively in therapy and clinical interpretation?

Answer: In an earlier volume (Schafer, 1976, pp. 42, 43, 49, 52) he advocated it very forcefully. In a later volume (Schafer, 1983, p. 245), however, he denied it and said that "it would be fatal to clinical exploration and effectiveness to do clinical work in that way."

Question: What are some of the applications of narration and action language in clinical interpretation that Schafer recommends?

Answer: He suggests (Schafer, 1983, pp. 248–257) the usefulness of regarding any act of thinking and speaking as an instance of narration. People learn not only how to compose and use these tales, but also how to act "in order to be able to give a coherent and continuous account of everyone's activities." Narratives of this kind concerning oneself make up a large part of such tales and become increasingly prominent and important to analyze in therapeutic discourse.

Question: What are some clinical examples of this concept?

Answer: Schafer (1983, p. 249) presents this clinical vignette:

CASE REPORT:

A male patient tells of having wanted to flirt with a married female colleague. He adds, "I didn't give in to myself." In this rendition he is giving a two-person narrative account of what, in action terms, could be presented as his having decided on a course of action that he did not altogether want to undertake. In his narrative, one person, with whom he consciously identifies, is insisting that he adhere to certain standards that he has set, while the other person is trying to overcome this opposition by insisting that the flirtatious course of action be undertaken. In portraying the action, in effect, as going on between two people in opposition to one another, he constructs the experience on the basis of what some psychoanalysts would call splitting of the self-representation.

In another example Schafer (1983, pp. 250–251) considers a self-reflexive term, *self-indulgence,* as in overeating. One might say, "I ate excessively according to the standards I maintain regarding quantity, and I contemplate what I did regretfully and contemptuously." In this action version of self-indulgence, rather than two selves being at odds with one another or at least interacting with one another, there is a single agent performing and considering certain of his or her actions in different, more or less incompatible ways. Clinically, depending on the dynamic context in which it appears, the therapist may retell a significant action such as overeating in many ways, for example, as nursing greedily, retreating from heterosexuality, or punishing oneself or others.

Question: How does Schafer interpret and deal with the frequent question by patients, "What should I talk about?"

Answer: Talking about something is a form of narration in which the patient encourages the therapist to expect a story of some kind. By establishing this narrative atmosphere, the patient attempts to define and thus also to limit what will be experienced. The patient is trying to establish a detached position as chronicler of events—contrary to the rule of free association. Although for technical reasons the therapist may decide not to intervene in this regard, he or she cannot listen to what is being told purely as story content. The therapist's highest priority must be an attempt to understand, in a depth-psychological way, the construction and communication of experience in the here and now of the therapy session. To achieve this understanding, the therapist must attend to the patient's selection and arrangement of what to talk about, the context and timing of it in the discourse, the style and manner in which the narration is performed, and the past and present meanings that may be inferred from the material.

Patients often come to their sessions with an opening topic that they have selected to talk about. It may be a report of the events of the day, a description of the mood they have been in, a rehearsed dream, or something else. One defensive function served by such an entrance is to avoid attending to the opening of the session itself—how it felt to come in and rejoin the therapist, how the therapist looked, or what would just come to mind. A similar function is served by silent or conspicuous preparation for the end of the session, for example, choosing not to say certain things because there is not enough time to talk about them (Schafer, 1983, pp. 251–255).

Question: These views by Schafer sound very much like those of classical approaches. Is he basically Freudian in his interpretive approach?

Answer: In many ways, yes, especially with respect to his use of clinical psychoanalytic theories in interpreting clinical narratives. He writes (Schafer, 1983, p. 187):

> The analyst is working with narrative performances . . . in formulating interpretations; and the confrontations and clarifications that lead up to interpretations may be said to be engaging in acts of retelling or narrative revision. The concept of retelling subsumes four overlapping terms: redescribing, reinterpreting, recontextualizing, and reducing. These terms overlap . . . because a description or interpretation makes sense only in some context within which it attains distinctiveness, relevance and significance . . . and from this it follows that reinterpretation necessarily recontextualizes that which it is designed to make more intelligible . . . And retelling requires reduction of meaning to the confining terms of another narrative.

Question: Example regarding clinical interpretation?

Answer: In an interpretation dealing with reaction formation against sadism, the therapist redescribes ostensible kindness as a defensive move; reinterprets as defensiveness what the patient considered and presented evidence of sheer kindness; recontextualizes ostensible kindness by placing it in a setting of infantile as well as current danger situations; or reduces the manifest forms and occasions of forced kindness to prototypic childhood situations of danger and defense (e.g., being good out of fear of abandonment).

Question: How is Schafer the most classical in his approach?

Answer: In this way: "In interpreting or retelling the analysand's narrative performances, the analyst follows certain storylines of personal development, conflictual situations, and subjective experience that are the distinguishing features of his or her analytic theory and approach" (Schafer, 1983, pp. 188–189). In addition, "there can be no theory-free and method-free facts. The purported life-historical facts that are initially presented by analysands become *psychoanalytic* facts only after they have been systematically retold by the analyst, who, it must be added, is more and more . . . joined in this project by the analysand as the analysis progresses. One might say that in the end the interpretations must be seen as coauthored" (Schafer, 1983, pp. 187–189).

Question: Does Schafer have any reservations about his extensive use of psychoanalytic theory in interpretations?

Answer: Some, but not many. About the reductive aspect of interpretations, he says (Schafer, 1983, p. 189) that it is not to be deplored but is inherent in tracing significant themes or developmental sequences in psychoanalysis. Regarding the latter, however, he notes the adultomorphic aspect of making interpretations of experience in early childhood—which again, however, he says is not to be deplored:

> Adultomorphism is involved, for example, when reference is made to infantile feelings and fantasies of "rejection," "abandonment," "starvation," or "loss of self (or self-boundaries)." These terms for infantile experience are not in accord with any known developmental–psychological account of cognition in early childhood. But the analysand's infantile modes and contents of experience can only become analytic data in formulations that necessarily recognize and enhance the continuing activity of both the analyst's and the analysand's "observing ego" or "mature psyche." One may say of analytic interpretation, therefore, that, far from unearthing and resurrecting old and archaic experiences as such, it constitutes and develops new, vivid, verbalizable, and verbalized versions of those experiences. Only then can these new versions be given a secure place in a continuous, coherent, convincing, and up-to-date psychoanalytic life history. This is the history that facilitates personal change and further development.

Question: To what else does Schafer attribute change or cure in his therapeutic and interpretive approach?

Answer: He states (Schafer, 1983, p. 190):

> Interpretation refines and stabilizes the way in which the analysand experiences his or her personal agency, especially in relation to what have come to be defined, through inter-

pretation, as critical life situations, such as the danger situations outlined by Freud [1926]. . . . Refined and stabilized personal agency is one way—the action language way—of referring to what is more familiarly known as increased autonomy of adaptive, self-reflective, and synthesizing ego functions . . . Personal agency is refined and stabilized by the analyst's insightful retelling of both disclaiming and excessive claiming of agency . . . In the reductive emphasis on repetition that characterizes analytic interpretation, the analyst steadily attributes agency to the analysand against sheer victimization . . . the great extent to which the analysand is unconsciously the agent or author of his or her life gets to be established beyond doubt.

REFERENCES

Freud, S. (1926). Inhibitions, symptoms and anxiety. *Standard edition* (Vol. 20, 77–178). London: Hogarth, 1959.

Schafer, R. (1976). A new language for psychoanalysis. New Haven, CT: Yale University Press.

——. (1983). The analytic attitude. New York: Basic Books.

Chapter 11

Spence's Radical Narrative Approach

Question: Why is Spence's narrative approach called radical?

Answer: Because he has mounted such a far-reaching critique of psychoanalysis and clinical interpretation, claiming, for example, that clinical interpretations are based less on fact than on fiction, and that the therapist's interpretations are merely narratives that have no evidential value but only rhetorical appeal (Spence, 1982, p. 32). In addition, he questions the concept of an unconscious mind, which he considers only a metaphor (Spence, 1987, p. 41)—"little more than sophisticated demonology." His overall critique of Freud and psychoanalysis is that "The Emperor has no clothes." For example, he attacks psychoanalytic ideas that have achieved iconic, publically unquestioned status. What a well-known analyst claims to "hear in the background" of his patients' associations, that is, detects as evidence of unconscious motivation, is really projected onto the material. Actual psychoanalytic data, he claims, are "scandalously unavailable." He uses these criticisms as a basis for arguing that psychoanalytic theory has remained relatively unchanged for almost one hundred years and that instead of a "grammar of early development" we have only a "literature of anecdotes, a dumping ground of observations which have little more evidential value than a 30-year-old collection of flying saucer reports."

Question: On what does Spence base his view that clinical interpretations are only narratives and have little or no basis in actual events?

Answer: He draws heavily on the writings of Loch and Viderman who distinguish between truth as historical fact that only discovery will bring to the surface and truth as "the construction of something that makes sense" (Loch, 1977). Viderman (1979) postulates that archaic experiences of early childhood

> have no structure, no figurable shape. Only interpretative speech can shape them and endow them with a new representation of what no longer exists except in a splintered, fragmented, unrecognizable form. Speech provides a denomination that unifies and concretizes them in a totally original way and in a form that exists nowhere in the unconscious of the patient, or anywhere else but in the analytic space through the language that provides it with form.

Question: What is meant by "the analytic space"?

Answer: It is a synonym for the therapeutic situation.

170

Question: Does Spence cite any clinical illustrations of Viderman's and Loch's concepts in this regard?

Answer: Yes, Viderman's (1979, p. 265) best-known clinical example:

CASE REPORT:

One of his patients reported the following dream: "My father and I are in a garden. I pick some flowers and offer him a bouquet of six roses." In an attempt to bring out the patient's ambivalent feelings toward his father, Viderman tried to combine the positive connotations of the gift with the negative feelings he may have had about the fact that his father had died of alcoholism. He took advantage of the phonetic similarity between the six roses of the dream and his father's fatal illness—cirrhosis of the liver (the similarity in sound connecting *six roses* and *cirrhosis* is particularly evident in French)—and made the following intervention: "Six roses or cirrhosis?" (Spence, 1982, p. 178) Viderman's explanatory comments are that the interpretation produced a new representation, and if the transference at the time allowed the interpretation to be accepted and integrated the construction would become true through the dynamic process that created it.

Question: What does Spence suggest should replace the classical concept of attempting to discover historical facts?

Answer: Aesthetic and pragmatic models of interpretation. For example, Viderman expresses the belief that the depth-psychological therapist functions more as a poet than a historian. He also argues that to be therapeutic an interpretation need have no connection with the patient's past. By choosing the right word, metaphor, or quotation to illustrate his point, the therapist may initiate a train of associations that leads to new discoveries. Loch emphasizes a pragmatic criterion of interpretive value and truth: what is fruitful is true. Constructions do not discover truth in the form of correspondence between facts of the past and interpretations concerning the past. Rather, on the basis of mutual agreement between the patient and the therapist, it constructs truth in the service of self-coherence for the present and the future.

Question: Does Spence conclude that interpretations are useless?

Answer: No. He writes (Spence, 1982, p. 163):

> Yet interpretations work—and perhaps that is the greatest puzzle. They have a certain compelling quality even in the face of obvious errors of reasoning and judgment . . . There is a satisfaction in seeing a tangled life reduced to a relatively small number of organized principles; satisfaction in seeing a previous explanation (e.g., the primal scene) come to life again in new circumstances; and finally, satisfaction in finding correspondence between events that are separated in time and space. There is no doubting the aesthetic value of these . . . satisfactions.

172

He cautions, however, that "The most serious mistake is to assume that good narrative fit indicates a bona fide discovery—whereas it is not a true discovery, but only a plausible fiction."

Question: Does Spence present any examples of the usefulness of narrative interpretations even though they are only "plausible fictions"?

Answer: Spence cites an observation by Annie Reich (1973, p. 350) of a student she supervised who, in response to his patient's dream, suddenly visualized the inscrutable smile of Mona Lisa. When the student communicated this (countertransference) image to the patient, a great deal of new material came to light. The image thus served as an interpretation that confirms its correctness by stimulating new material.

Question: Does Spence equate narrative interpretations with persuasion?

Answer: Yes. He (Spence, 1982, p. 270) writes that coherence and completeness are necessary but not sufficient: "An important ingredient of the power to persuade is the aesthetic nature of the narrative. As with any good story, form is as important as content."

Question: How does Spence conceptualize the process of narratives, as "plausible fictions," becoming true?

Answer: He is not entirely clear on this point, but says: "Associations and interpretations, as they are inserted into the developing narrative, become true, as they become familiar and lend meaning to otherwise disconnected pieces of the patient's life" (Spence, 1982, p. 280). This seems to imply that the growing familiarity with and usefulness of the narrative give it the status of "truth."

Question: Does Spence consider interpretations 100 percent narrative?

Answer: Almost, but not quite. He acknowledges that interpretations are never "zero-based" historically or 100 percent narrative, but at the same time he advocates (Spence, 1987, p. 280) a "new brand of 'tough-minded hermeneutics' which assumes that no pattern exists [in the patient's mind] until it is discovered . . . that no regularities can be assumed until they have been established beyond reasonable doubt." His way of attempting to assess "reasonable doubt" draws on the judicial–legal metaphor proposed by Runyon (1982), who suggests that different parties have competing interests in aspects of psychoanalytic theory. Both psychoanalysis and the law depend on procedures that are rule governed but not rule bound, influenced as much by the circumstances of a particular happening as by an abstract set of laws—a view requiring that cases be described in maximal detail. Then the cases should be subjected to the legal tradition of peer commentary, with its metaphor of "discovery through dialogue"—an accumulation of commentaries, differing readings of the same situation, and the accumulating overlay of new contexts, in place of the metaphor of excavating a singular cause.

Question: What is Spence's explanation of the consensus problem—the difficulty that therapists have in agreeing on the interpretation of the same case material?

Answer: His explanation, which leaves out the numerous inherent difficulties of interpretive work, is simply that each interpreter is making up his or her own "story." To be consistent in his argument, Spence is also forced to question the concepts of thematic unity and the hierarchy of meanings in clinical material.

Question: What are some further clinical examples of Spence's approach?

Answer: In his 1987 book *The Freudian Metaphor: Toward Paradigm Change in Psychoanalysis* (p. 60), a patient begins to describe an incident in her kitchen: "I was cutting some liverwurst, and I noticed that the thick skin around it and all made me think of a penis or something like a snake." The analyst replies: "And you were eating it." On quick reading this seems like a non sequitur and a good example of leading the witness, but a little further thought suggests that the analyst was working with a particular metaphor in mind—the popular fantasy of incorporating the phallus—and in the context of this model his reply makes perfect sense. But notice the difference from the standard fomulation: we are not saying that the meaning of the kitchen incident was contained in the material, but rather that it (arose from and) became clear when it was heard within the bounds of a particular metaphor. Whether or not this was true or even relevant becomes a separate issue.

175

In the next example (pp. 55–56), Spence expresses his strong reservations about the method of listening with "evenly suspended attention," which he claims perpetuates the myth that the analyst is hearing only what is "there" and is in no sense participating in the construction of meaning. The example is from Dewald's (1972, p. 175) book, *The Psychoanalytic Process*. The patient is talking about a dream in which she was in a playpen with other girls, dressed up in frilly dresses but wearing no pants. A group of men were looking down at them. In her associations, the patient turns to thoughts of the analyst and says, "You are capable of loving me and of not caring what I look like, and for you it wouldn't make any difference about the . . ." There was a sixty-second silence, and then the analyst said, "You cut something off there." The patient replied, "The surface things." The analyst then interpreted, "I think you mean the presence or absence of a penis."

Spence asks: "Was that what the patient meant? Other possibilities come to mind—frilly clothes or the fact that she was wearing no pants—but Dewald seems bent on just one reading of the material, and the thrust of his standard interpretation is anticipated by his comment, "You cut something off there." (If castration is on his mind, then the phrase "cut something off" already alerts us to the specific meanings that will be projected onto the material.) In the minds of some analysts, this interchange would be an example of evenly suspended attention. They would say that because he is in a state of evenly suspended attention he is able to detect the latent castration theme and make the interpretation. I would suggest that something much less mystical is going on, namely, that the analyst projected a standard interpretative model onto the material and that this projection operates outside of [the analyst's] awareness . . . [and] it should also be noted that the castration model forecloses other kinds of understanding.

For another example of how observation cannot be divorced from theory, consider the following anecdote from Brenner (1982, p. 172) concerning a patient who, he felt, had been "overwhelmed by penis envy since childhood" (pp. 81–82):

> As another illustration of how she felt about being without a penis, she came into my office one day indignant because, when she had gone to use the lavatory just before, she had found the toilet seat up. "No one," she said, "has any right to leave a toilet seat in that position." "Why not?" I asked. "Because," she said, "it looks so ugly that way." She explained that she had always felt one of the ugliest things in the world is a toilet with the seat up. If the lid or the seat were down, it looked presentable, but she could never stand the way it looked with the seat up.

Spence asks: Does the unpleasant sight of open toilet seats stem from an envy of men and all their rights and privileges (including the right to urinate while standing), or does it stem from a much more complicated set of considerations? Interior decorators who design matching covers for toilet seats would be affronted by the sight of an open seat—for purely aesthetic reasons. From another point of view, an open seat brings into view the contents of the bowl, and under certain conditions, that is better left unseen. From the standpoint of pure form, a lifted seat spoils the symmetry of design and detracts from its overall appearance, much as an automobile is uglier with its hood up or its trunk open.

With these considerations in mind, it seems apparent that the interchange with the patient has more than one meaning. It is no longer a transparent piece of data (similar to a meter reading) whose significance is immediately clear to all observers and whose meaning can be readily detached from its context. Brenner may be entirely right in his interpretation, but the outside reader will not be convinced unless he is given a vast amount of additional data about this particular patient—and these data are not supplied.

The following example (pp. 195–197) is a fragment from Case C, presented by Gill and Hoffman. The patient, an actress, is talking to her analyst about some problems with (J), her director:

> P: Yes, sort of, except I—I know that. I think one thing that he resents about it is that he knows I'm—this may sound weird—but he knows I'm talking to somebody else instead of talking to him. And the reason I think that is because he likes to know what everybody's up to and he likes to, you know, know where they're at. And I think he considers it like a threat to him. Just the way he considers, you know, my talking to G about things a threat. Anytime anybody makes, you know, yells at the top of their lungs about my seeing a shrink, I don't like it. I was very embarrassed when T said it. I mean it's not something I'm particularly proud of, you know. (Pause) You know, with people, with people I know, it's cool but—or with people that I feel comfortable with I guess is a better thing. And I guess what it is, is people that I think are going to stick with me till I get fixed, you see. I remember the thing I didn't like about T saying it was that it's like I assumed that everybody else would say, "Oh, we wouldn't, we're not going to have to pay attention to her, you know. Poor crazy girl."

> Analyst: "She doesn't have anything worth paying attention to."

> P: "All right, if you want to put it that way. Or did I already put it that way? You know, I'm getting sick of this. Every time we come back to the same thing and then just stops there. Mental block. Done this routine many times before, I'm thinking of knocking all the books off the wall again. So what about it?"

Commentaries

By Gill and Hoffman (1982) (investigators of this therapeutic process):

> The analyst now more clearly refers to the female genital ["she had nothing worth paying attention to"]. The patient's response provides us with data which make plausible the inference that the earlier material about the dictatorial man alludes to the analyst implicitly. Even her saying, "All right, if you want to put it that way," suggests that she feels he insists on directing every detail [like her director]. She is sick of what she experiences as his reiterating this point which still leaves her "in the dark"—i.e., does not contribute to her progress in dealing with the issue. She responds with an angry wish to knock his books off the wall, perhaps because she feels he is mechanically following some formula taken right from a book.

Analyst's commentary:

> (Some minutes later the treating analyst commented: "I take the idea about knocking all the books off the wall as if you wanted to knock my penis off.")

Additional commentary by Gill and Hoffman:

> An almost unbelievably pat interpretation that exemplifies our point. Instead of finding out what she means by wanting to knock down his books, the analyst uses what she has said to reiterate his fixed conviction, which—however correct it may be—she has just characterized as unhelpful. It is far more likely that her conscious experience is that he is repeating a formula from his books and that that is why she wants to knock them down.

Spence's commentary:

> The emphasis on being crazy and getting fixed make it sound as if the patient is more concerned with being thought mentally ill than being found defective (castrated), and the analyst, in his eagerness to give the material a standard interpretation, may have overlooked the former in preference for the latter. The second excerpt is equally ambiguous. Does the wish to knock his books off the wall refer to taking pat interpretations from books (as Gill and Hoffman suggest), or does it have a more private meaning? This is not the first time she has had the thought; what was its first context and does that give us more insight into its meaning?

Present author's commentary:

These examples from Spence's writings illustrate that, despite his radical critique of psychoanalysis and his radical views about interpretations representing narratives that are nothing but "plausible fictions," his ways of dealing with clinical material suggest that his aim is not to tear down psychoanalysis and clinical interpretation but to improve them.

REFERENCES

Brenner, C. (1982). *The mind in conflict.* New York: International Universities Press.

Dewald, P. (1972). *The psychoanalytic process.* New York: Basic Books.

Gill, M., & Hoffman, I. (1982). *Analysis of transference: Vol. II, studies of nine audio-recorded psychoanalytic sessions.* New York: International Universities Press.

Loch, W. (1977). Some comments on the subject of psychoanalysis and truth. In J. Smith (Ed.), *Thought, consciousness, and reality* (pp. 217–255). New Haven, CT: Yale University Press.

Reich, A. (1973). *Annie Reich: Psychoanalytic contributions.* New York: International Universities Press.

Runyon, W. (1982). In defense of the case study method. *American Journal of Orthopsychiatry, 52,* 440–446.

Spence, D. (1982). *Narrative truth and historical truth: Meaning and interpretation in psychoanalysis.* New York: Norton.

Spence, D. (1987). *The Freudian metaphor: Toward paradigm change in psychoanalysis.* New York: Norton.

Viderman, S. (1979). The analytic space: Meaning and problems. *Psychoanalytic Quarterly, 48,* 257–291.

Chapter 12

The Intersubjective Approach

Question: What is meant clinically by *intersubjective?*

Answer: The interplay of the two differently organized subjective "worlds" of patient and therapist, in the continuously shifting psychological field created by their interaction.

Question: Is this approach associated with any particular authors?

Answer: Yes, especially Robert Stolorow (1988) and his co-workers (Stolorow & Atwood, 1992; Stolrow, Brandschaft, & Atwood, 1992); but a number of other writers are also prominently associated with the intersubjective school, for example, Thomas Ogden (1994), Owen Renik (1993), and others.

Question: What is meant by *subjective worlds?*

Answer: Stolorow and other subjectivists envision only one kind of reality—one that is completely subjective. The subjective world with which they are concerned is the reality of subjective experience, both felt and perceived, mediated through interaction with others (including the therapeutic relationship and interaction).

Question: How does this concept apply to the treatment situation?

Answer: These authors maintain that the therapeutic process is inherently an intersubjective one. They have sought to demonstrate in detail that clinical phenomena such as transference and countertransference, negative therapeutic reaction, psychopathology in general, and the therapeutic action of psychoanalysis cannot be understood apart from the specific intersubjective contexts in which they take form.

Question: Do these authors take external reality into account?

Answer: In an evaluation of the intersubjective approach, Moore (1999, p. 18) writes: "Within the narrow range of reality that intersubjective theory considers, the sole concept of external reality is the intersubjective field."

Question: What is an example of Moore's statement?

Answer: Moore (1999, p. 78) writes further: "No example of the narrowness of this focus is more striking than when trauma to a patient is explored. Sometimes no allowance appears to be made for the sheer independent impact of an externally imposed catastrophe." Instead, Stolorow and Atwood (1992) appear to locate the basis of traumatic stress exclusively in the lack of sympathetically and attuned social contact that accompany and precede it. For example, lack of preparation for trauma by "early faulty attunement" is frequently held to blame; that is, it is a failure of the early intersubjective field:

> Trauma is viewed here not as an event or a series of events overwhelming an ill-equipped "psychic appraratus." Rather, the tendency for affective experience to create a disorganized (i.e., traumatic) self state is seen to originate from early faulty affect attunement, with a lack of mutual sharing and acceptance of affect states, leading to impaired affect tolerance and inability to use affect as self-signals (Stolorow et al., 1987, p. 72).

Question: This sounds somewhat similar to self psychology, with its emphasis on affect attunement, self states, and so forth. Is there such a connection?

Answer: Yes, Stolorow (1983, 1986, 1995) has indicated that his intersubjective approach draws on and attempts to extend self psychology (see also Goldberg's [1998] paper in which he

185

refers to intersubjectivity as one of the three major post-Kohutian schools that compete for influence in self psychology).

Question: What is an example of applying the intersubjective approach in the clinical situation?

Answer: A brief example is not possible because clinicians of the intersubjective school report not only what is going on in the patient during therapy sessions but also a detailed account of their own subjective thoughts, feelings, and sensations, including aspects of their own life histories. The case report that I have chosen to cite is from Ogden (1994, pp. 13–16):

CASE REPORT:

A 42-year-old married lawyer and mother of two latency-aged children came to analysis for reasons that were not clear originally. Despite having a "wonderful family" and doing well in her work, she felt a vague discontent with her life. The first year-and-a-half of analysis had a belaboured and unsettling feeling to it. She spoke in an organized, somewhat obsessional but thoughtful way; and there were always important themes to discuss, for example, her mother's jealousy about even small amounts of attention paid to her by her father. There was a superficiality to this, however, and as time went on she had more and more difficulty "finding things to talk about." She spoke of feeling "not fully present" at the sessions, in spite of her best efforts to "be there."

By the end of the second year of analysis the silences had become increasingly frequent and considerably longer in duration, often lasting 15 to 20 minutes. She repeatedly apologized for not having more to say and worried that she was failing the therapist. As the months passed, there was a growing feeling of exhaustion and despair associated with the silences and the overall lifelessness of the analysis. The therapist's fantasies and daydreams were unusually sparse during this period of the work; and one morning while driving to work and thinking of the people he would be seeing that day, he could not remember this particular patient's first name. He imagined himself as a mother who, because of profound ambivalence concerning her baby, was unable to give the baby a name after its birth.

During this period the therapist developed what he felt was a mild case of the "flu," but he was able to keep his appointments with all of his patients. In the weeks that followed, he noticed that he continued to feel physically unwell during his sessions with this patient, experiencing malaise, nausea, and vertigo. He was not aware of such feelings while seeing his other patients. He concluded that the sessions with this patient must be particularly draining for him, and that the long silences in her sessions allowed him to be more self-conscious about his physical state.

Next, he began to feel a diffuse anxiety during his sessions with her; and he noted that before the sessions he would delay the moment when he would have to meet her in the waiting room—by making phone calls, sorting papers, etc. Occasionally he would be a minute or so late in beginning her session. One day when he leaned over to take a sip from a glass of water beside his chair, the patient startled him by abruptly (for the first time in the analysis) turning around on the couch to look at him. She had a look of panic on her face and said: "I'm sorry. I didn't know what was happening to you." At that point the therapist experienced a feeling of terror—that something catastrophic was happening to him. He then became aware that the anxiety he had been feeling and his (predominantly unconscious) dread of the sessions with her (reflected in his procrastinating behavior about her sessions) were directly connected with an unconscious sensation/fantasy that his somatic symptoms were caused by her—that she was killing him.

The therapist understood at this point that for several weeks he had been emotionally consumed by the unconscious conviction that he had a serious illness, perhaps a brain tumor, and had been afraid that he was dying. He felt great relief as he came to understand these thoughts, feelings, and sensations as reflections of transference–countertransference events occurring in this analysis. Referring to her turning to him in fright, he told her that he thought she had been afraid that something terrible was happening and that he might even be dying. She said that when she heard him moving in his chair she had the fearful thought that he was having a heart attack. She added that for some time she had felt he looked ashen, but had not wanted to worry him by saying so. (Her ability to speak to him about her perceptions, feelings, and fantasies in this way suggested that a significant psychological shift had begun to occur.) The therapist's and patient's capacities to think as separate individuals had been co-opted by the intensity of the shared unconscious fantasy/somatic delusion in which both had been enmeshed.

The therapist interpreted further to the patient that not only was she afraid he was dying, but that she was afraid she was the cause of his condition—that just as recently she was worried that she was having a damaging effect on her son and had taken him to the doctor, she was afraid also that she was making the therapist so ill that he would die. She said that what they were talking about felt true to her in an important way, but she worried that she would forget it all after her session that day. Her comment reminded the therapist of his having forgotten her first name, and his fantasy of being a mother unwilling to acknowledge fully the birth of her baby. The therapist now felt that their respective ambivalences toward each other reflected a fear, jointly held by patient and therapist, that allowing her "to be born" (i.e., to become genuinely alive and present) in the analysis would pose a serious danger to both of them. They had created an unconscious fantasy (generated largely in the form of bodily experience) that her coming to life (her birth) in the analysis would make the therapist ill and possibly kill him.

The therapist now interpreted to the patient that the reason she could not feel "present" in the therapist's office was because she was attempting to be invisible in her silence, and that by doing so she would be less of a strain on the therapist and prevent his becoming ill. She said this was a feeling she had had for as long as she could remember; for although her mother reassured her repeatedly that she had been thrilled to be pregnant with her and had looked forward to her birth, the patient felt convinced that she had been "a mistake" and that her mother had not wanted to have children. Her mother was in her late 30's and her father in his mid-40's when she was born; she was the only child, and as far as she knew there had been no other pregnancies. She felt guilty about saying so, but her parents' home did not feel to her like a place for children. This helped to account for the patient's effort in the analysis to behave "like an adult," and not make an emotional "mess" of the therapist's "home" (the analysis) by strewing

it with infantile and irrational thoughts, feelings and behavior. Unconsciously, she had been torn between her
need to get help from the therapist and her fear that the
very act of claiming a place for herself with him ("in him")
would deplete or kill him. The therapist now understood
his fantasy (and associated sensory experiences) of having
a brain tumor as a reflection of an unconscious fantasy that
the patient's very existence was a kind of growth that
greedily, selfishly, and destructively took up space in him
where it did not belong.

During these exchanges, for the first time the therapist
felt that there were two people in the room talking to one
another. Not only was the patient able to think and talk
more fully as a living human being, but also the therapist
felt that he was thinking, feeling, and experiencing sensation in a way that had a quality of realness and spontaneity
of which he had not been capable previously with this
patient.

Question: How do intersubjectivists justify the extent to which
they are preoccupied with their own subjectivities during patients'
sessions?

Answer: They claim that the therapist's experience in and of
the intersubjective process is primarily that of a vehicle for the
understanding of conscious and unconscious experiences of the
patient. The unconscious experience of the patient is privileged
in a specific way; that is, it is the past and present experience of
the patient that is taken to be the principal subject of the
therapeutic discourse. (Thus the intersubjective experience of

patient and therapist is asymmetrical because the patient and therapist are not engaged in a democratic process of mutual analysis.)

Another form of justification for the extent to which intersubjectivists focus on their own subjectivities during therapy sessions is the following: the basic precondition for empathic communication is the therapist's own personal knowledge of the type of experience the patient is reporting. Whatever the patient reports, the therapist "has been there" at some point in his or her life. Thus to understand the patient's report the therapist must draw subjectively on a recognition of a similar experience in his or her own life (Singer, 1977, p. 183; cited by Renik, 1995).

Ogden writes (1994, pp. 12–13) as follows about his extensive and deep intersubjective "immersion" in the case cited above:

> I believe that a major dimension of the analyst's psychological life in the consulting room with the patient takes the form of reverie concerning the ordinary details of his own life (that are often of great narcissistic importance to him) . . . These reveries are not simply reflections of inattentiveness, narcissistic self-involvement, unresolved emotional conflict, and the like; rather, this psychological activity represents symbolic and proto-symbolic (sensation-based) forms given to the unarticulated (and often not yet felt) experience of the patient as they are taking form in the intersubjectivity of the analytic pair.
>
> This form of psychological activity is often viewed as something the analyst must get through, put aside, overcome, etc. in his effort to be both emotionally present with and attentive to the analysand. I am suggesting that a view of the analyst's experience that dismisses this category of clinical fact leads the analyst to ignore (or diminish) the significance of a great deal (in some instances, the majority) of his experience with the patient. I feel that a principal factor that contributes to the undervaluation of such a large portion of the analytic experience is the fact that such acknowledgment involves a

disturbing form of self-consciousness [and self-disclosure?]. This aspect of the transference–countertransference requires an examination of the way we talk to ourselves and what we talk to ourselves about in a private, relatively undefended psychological state . . . In becoming self-conscious in this way, we are tampering with an essential inner sanctuary of privacy, and therefore with one of the cornerstones of our sanity.

The realm of transference–countertransference experience is so personal, so ingrained in the character structure of the analyst, that it requires a great deal of psychological effort to enter into a discourse with ourselves in a way that it requires . . . If we are to be analysts in a full sense, we must self-consciously attempt to bring even this aspect of ourselves to bear on the analytic process.

REFERENCES

Goldberg, A. (1998). Self psychology since Kohut. *Psychoanalytic Quarterly, 67*, 240–255.

Moore, R. (1999). *The creation of reality in psychoanalysis.* Hillsdale, NJ: Analytic Press.

Ogden, T. (1994). The analytic third: Working with intersubjective facts. *International Journal of Psychoanalysis, 75*, 3–19.

Renik, O. (1993). Analytic interaction: Conceptualizing technique in light of the analyst's irreducible subjectivity. *Psychoanalytic Quarterly, 62*, 553–571.

Singer, E. (1977). The fiction of psychoanalytic anonymity. In Ed. K. Frank, *The human dimension in psychoanalysis,* pp. 181–192. New York: Grune & Stratton.

Stolorow, R. (1983). Self psychology: A structural psychology. In J. Kichtenberg & S. Kaplan (Eds.), *Reflections on self psychology* (pp. 287–296). Hillsdale, NJ: Analytic Press.

Stolorow, R. (1986). Critical reflections on the theory of self psychology: An inside view. *Psychoanalytic Inquiry, 6*, 382–402.

Stolorow, R. (1988). Intersubjectivity, psychoanalytic knowing, and reality. *Contemporary Psychoanalysis, 24,* 331–338.

Stolorow, R. (1995). An intersubjective view of self psychology. *Psychoanalytic Dialogues, 5,* 393–400.

Stolorow, R., & Atwood, G. (1992). *Contexts of being: The intersubjective foundations of psychological life.* Hillsdale, NJ: Analytic Press.

Stolorow, R., Brandschaft, B., & Atwood, G. (1987). *Psychoanalytic treatment: An intersubjective approach.* Hillsdale, NJ: Analytic Press.

Chapter 13

The Radical Relational Approach

Question: What characterizes the radical relational approach developed by Greenberg and Mitchell (1993; Mitchell, 1988, 1998)?

Answer: Greenberg (2001, pp. 352–363) suggests that for the most part four premises are accepted by relational analysts:

1. The therapist influences the patient's experience in a myriad of ways. Much of what the patient thinks and feels is responsive to what the therapist does and even to who he or she is. Everything the therapist says (and much of what is not said) will affect the patient deeply.
2. The impact of the therapist's behavior can never be understood while it is happening. A great deal of work in every treatment is to understand, after the fact, what has transpired in an unexamined way between the patient and therapist.

3. There is no technical posture the therapist can adopt that will guarantee the creation of a predictable atmosphere in the treatment. Neutrality and abstinence are myths. Therapy can be conducted only in fits and starts, as a result of negotiations within each individual dyad—the aim of which is to find a way of working that is unique to the dyad and will suit both participants.

4. Even as an observer, the therapist's subjectivity is a ubiquitous presence in the treatment. Objectivity by the therapist is a myth. Opinions among relational therapists differ about whether the patient brings something—for example, an unconscious—that can be discovered and known, or whether all meanings are constructed on the basis of here-and-now relations between the patient and therapist.

Regarding the relational approach, Mitchell (1998) emphasizes that "any understanding of a mind, one's own or another's, is personal . . . one's own understanding":

> The analyst, if he or she is meaningfully engaged in the process, inevitably becomes touched and moved by the patient, and happily so. The understandings that emerge within the analyst's mind are embedded in the fluid, interpenetrating tapestry of their encounter, with their perpetual influence on each other . . . The analyst's conjectures about the patient are saturated with countertransferential responses to the patient. (p. 20)

Mitchell (1998) believes that Freud's most important contribution was not the specific *content* he ascribed to the unconscious at any particular time, but the discovery of an enriching *method* of explanation and meaning making. The relational shift is from classical oedipal explanations concerning sexual and aggressive conflicts to explanations concerning conflictual attachments and discordant self–other organizations in lived experience—reflected in relational events between the patient and therapist in the treatment.

Mitchell further adds that "The analyst's expertise lies, most fundamentally, in his or her understanding of a *process*—what happens when one person begins to express and reflect on his or her experience in the presence of a trained listener, in the highly structured context provided by the analytic situation."

Question: What is a clinical example of the relational approach?

Answer:

CASE REPORT:

Mitchell (1998, pp. 21–26) describes a 40-year-old corporate executive who sought treatment because he was tortured by bad dreams in which he felt swamped by tasks and demands on his time, and in which he would find that he had overlooked or forgotten some crucial detail, leading to disastrous consequences. He had a simple, unidimensional view of his own mind. His poor but happy parents had made enormous personal sacrifices to fund the education of their children. He considered his nightmares a reaction to the pressures of his work but could not understand why he was unable to handle the pressures with less anxiety.

Within the first several weeks of sessions it became clear that the affect in the dream vis-á-vis work-related pressures corresponded to a more general worry about his wife and children that he had suffered from for many years. He feared that he would become so absorbed in some project or distraction that he would not be available to them when they were endangered. He had particular concerns about his son, David (he also had two older daughters). He saw David as caught up in the greedy, television-inspired materialism of American culture and worried about how he would be able to instill in him the self-sacrificing devotion he learned from his own parents. He then reported his first dream in the analysis:

I am climbing down a stone wall in my backyard; David is with me. I am lowering him down to the ground by holding onto his arm. He was about a foot from the ground when I let him go. It should have been safe, but he punched a hole in the ground and sank into some kind of of chamber. He disappeared into the hole. There was some sort of light, as if there were a floor five or six feet below the ground. He bounced and rolled off to the side, so I couldn't see him. I started screaming for my wife to call the police, ambulance, something. I began digging frantically. I wasn't getting anywhere. There were sliding rocks. Then there were rescue workers, lots of people. There was a horrific feeling that David was dying. Then I noticed a piece of wood poking out of the dirt some distance away. It was moving. I dug down and uncovered a box like one of my filing boxes in which I keep all sorts of things I think I might need someday. I pulled the box up, and inside was David. He was alive and well.

Mitchell goes on to consider several features of the inter-action between the patient and himself around this dream: After exploring and developing many of his rich associa-tions to the dream, which included his chronic fear that his world and his mind might suddenly give way, I told him that I thought it might be understood to suggest that there were places in his mind that he was not aware of, in which pieces of his own experience had been placed for safekeeping and future reference. I also suggested that his struggles with his son were in some measure reflec-tive of struggles with a part of himself that had long been buried.

The patient began the next session by "complimenting" me on my "creative" understanding of the dream, by which it soon became clear he meant far-fetched. But he then told me another dream in which his wife (who has an interest in psychoanalysis and had encouraged him to enter treat-ment) suddenly disappeared into an elaborate system of underground pipes.

In his associations to this image, he recalled that the house in which his family had lived during his child-hood had a septic system underneath the backyard. The tank in this system would need to be drained periodically by a visiting truck, at considerable expense. To save money for the education of the children, his father undertook the massive project of digging trenches for lateral pipes to the tank, which would increase the available drainage underground. The children would be enlisted in these masssive digging projects. The patient remembered his mother's concern for his safety, since the trenches were at times deeper than he was tall. There was one memory in which he struck at some rocks with his shovel, and water from an underground spring began to fill the trench.

But he was pulled to safety before the trench filled with water.

Question: What was Mitchell's interpretation of this material?

Answer:

CASE REPORT:

Through the lens of relational psychoanalytic theory, one can see that [the patient's] conscious, isolated sense of himself is embedded within a complex network of relationships within his own mind of which he is largely unaware. His father, whom he remembers only lovingly, was internalized by him in a complex fashion. There is a part of him, a greedy, aggressive part of him . . . , that had been buried in his father's world of devotion and hard work. The sector of his experience that was buried and remains dissociated seems to correspond to and resonate with his son and his typical childish egotism and greediness. He becomes involved in desperate efforts to control his son, partly because the son stands also for the version of himself that he has long since entombed and which he deeply fears. Yet his dreams of something important that has been forgotten suggest to me that he is struggling with a sense that he has tragically mutilated his own inner resources and potentials (Mitchell, 1998, pp. 21–22).

Question: Does Mitchell consider his interpretation the only possible one?

Answer: No. He states that this is just one way of understanding the material and that there are no doubt many others. He adds, however, that

> To be primarily occupied with figuring out what the dream "really means" is to miss the point. Dream interpretation must be in the service of facilitating the analytic process . . . [and] for me the analytic process is about expanding and enriching the patient's experience of his own mind and facilitating his capacity to generate experience that he finds vitalizing and personally meaningful. From this perspective, arriving at a "best guess" [through] decoding the dream is neither possible nor desirable; what is important is engaging him about the dream in a way that sparks and quickens his own analytic interest in himself (Mitchell, 1998, pp. 23–24).

Question: How does Mitchell's viewpoint differ from the classical approach to interpretation?

Answer: There is no difference in the goal of furthering the therapeutic process, but the two approaches differ in how to achieve that goal. The classical approach places more emphasis on the importance and value of "correct" interpretations, that is, the "most plausible construction" at a given time in facilitating the therapeutic process—which Mitchell considers both impossible and undesirable.

Question: What other differences between the two approaches can be seen in Mitchell's case report?

Answer: One is how early in the therapy his interaction with the patient includes fairly extensive suggestions about the meaning of the first dream in the treatment. In the classical approach the therapist is much more circumspect about making interpretations so early in a treatment. Another difference is his assumption that what seems clear to him will be equally clear to the reader. For example, he commented that "Within the first several weeks of sessions it becomes clear that the affect in the dream vis-á-vis work-related pressures corresponds to a more general worry about his wife and children that he had suffered from for many years" (Mitchell, 1998, p. 22). In another example he states: "He began the next session by complimenting me on my 'creative' understanding of the dream, by which it soon became clear he meant far-fetched" (Mitchell, 1998, p. 23). Still another example: "Through the lens of relational psychoanalytic theory, one can see that [the patient's] conscious, isolated sense of himself is embedded within a complex network of relationships within his own mind of which he is largely unaware."

It is possible, of course, that what he inferred was correct, but to assume that other clinicians would see the material as (clearly as) he did is an example of what in the classical approach is called the transparency fallacy—assuming that the latent meanings in a set of clinical data are "transparent" to anyone who observes the data. This fallacy is prone to occur in connection with tendentious arguments by the therapist.

Question: What is a good article evaluating the relational approach of Greenberg and Mitchell?

202

A**nswer:**   Somewhat surprisingly and ironically, Greenberg (2001) himself recently published an evaluation of the very method that he helped to develop. He notes that

> despite the openness of relational theory, many of the most influential clinical vignettes in the recent literature emphasize the analyst's risk-taking, engaging patients in a highly personal way that breaks the traditional analytic frame. Various implications of the tendency for relational analysts to emphasize this sort of intervention are discussed, and questions are raised about the way this may affect how relational thinking is received. (Greenberg, 2001, p. 359)

He concludes even more trenchantly with the following remarks (Greenberg, 2001, pp. 379–380):

> Let me conclude by recalling the way that medieval morality plays worked. The plays were designed to inflame the audience's desire to reject evil and do good. I am struck by the similar tone of contemporary relational vignettes. The characters are different, of course. Instead of gluttony, lechery, sloth, hope, and charity, today we have rigidity, authoritarianism, orthodoxy, openness, decentering, and negotiability. But the endings of the plays and the vignettes are strikingly the same; both end optimistically, with the saving of the protagonist's soul. The message of the vignettes is that saving our psychoanalytic souls depends on finding the right way of being with our patients. But, like the morality plays, there is a great deal of excess in these reports, and like the plays their message can be oppressive. I hope that by taking this beginning look at some of this excess, I have opened the way to a new dialogue that will allow us to realize the potential of relational thinking while helping us avoid becoming the sort of movement that forecloses possibilities.

Another critique of Mitchell's approach has been published recently by Eagle, Wolitzky, and Wakefield (2001).

Question: Is there any relation between the relational and intersubjective approaches?

Answer: Yes, at least in theory. In Mitchell's (2000) last book, *Relationality: From Attachment to Intersubjectivity*, he proposes four modes, or "dimensions," of an interactional hierarchy through which relationality is expressed. These four modes or dimensions include "nonreflective behavior" (implicit mutual influence and regulation of interactions with one another), "affective permeability" (shared emotional states), "self-other configurations" (affectively tinged cognitive representations of the self and other), and "intersubjectivity" (the "mutual recognition of self-reflective agentic persons"). These several modes increase in "organizational sophistication" from the first to the last.

REFERENCES

Eagle, M., Wolitzky, D., & Wakefield, J. (2001). The analyst's knowledge and authority: A critique of the "new view" in psychoanalysis. *Journal of the American Psychoanalytic Association, 49*, 457–491.

Greenberg, J. (2001). The analyst's participation: A new look. *Journal of the American Psychoanalytic Association, 49*, 359–380.

Greenberg, J., & Mitchell, S. (1983). *Object Relations in Psychoanalysis*. Cambridge, MA: Harvard University Press.

Mitchell, S. (1988). *Relational concepts in psychoanalysis*. Cambridge, MA: Harvard University Press.

Mitchell, S. (1998). The analyst's knowledge and authority. *Psychoanalytic Quarterly, 67*, 1–31.

Mitchell, S. (2000). *Relationality: From attachment to intersubjectivity*. Hillsdale, NJ: Analytic Press.

Chapter 14

Pluralistic Approaches

Question: What is meant by *pluralistic approaches?*

Answer: Interpretive approaches that include both classical and various postclassical concepts and methods. For example, Fred Busch (2001, p. 740), who is generally considered a staunch classicist, writes:

> The landscape of psychoanalytic thought has dramatically changed with the infusion of insights from theoretical schools that highlight the role of relationships (internal, external, projected, selfobject, analytic, etc.) in the formation and amelioration of psychic conflict. These schools encompass the relational, social constructivist, interpersonal, intersubjective, object relations, and self-psychological perspectives (see Aron, 1996, for a succinct summary of these). Their insights have enriched our knowledge and added yet another dimension to the subtlety of our understanding of the effects of significant relationships in human development, the complex ways that these are integrated and translated into human behavior, and

how they—especially in the analytic relationship—may affect the tone and shape of all analyses.

Question: Does Busch acknowledge his pluralistic approach to clinical interpretation?

Answer: Yes. Responding to a critical commentary on the preceding essay, he said, "I am in complete agreement . . . on the significance of Loewald's work for understanding our patients—and also Kohut's, Kernberg's, Aron's, Mitchell's, and others too many to mention. When it comes to understanding our patients I am a theoretical pluralist, and I'm not sure what led [to the comment] that I'm interested only in drives and defenses" (Busch, 2001, p. 777).

Question: What is the common ground that makes such combined approaches possible?

Answer: The therapist's attempt to understand the mind of the patient in depth. Theodore Jacobs (2001) suggests, for example, that postclassical concepts and methods are an addition to—not a substitute for—the classic focus on defense and transference analysis. Understanding of the therapist's subjectivity, the patient's effect on it, and its effect on the patient opens a further channel to the unconscious of the patient. Thus, countertransference and the intersubjective perspective offer an additional tool in depth-psychological work. If the therapist were to limit his or her approach to investigating only the patient's material, it would close off a potentially valuable approach to understanding the patient's unconscious. Jacobs adds, "Such a perspective . . . in no way distracts from the inner world of the patient. In fact, it often provides access that is obtainable in no other way" (p. 756).

Question: What about the view that meaning is exclusively constructed in the therapeutic process? Can it be combined with the classical and other approaches?

Answer: Yes, if the word *exclusively* is omitted. To assume that meaning is created exclusively in the therapeutic process would deny that patients' suffering is largely the result of long-standing maladaptive beliefs and fantasies. Irwin Hoffman (1998), a leading spokesperson for the constructivist perspective, emphasizes that there is a continual dialectic between old internalized beliefs and new knowledge that develops in the course of treatment—between meanings that are revealed and those that are engendered. Bollas (1997, p. 336) cogently describes how the two approaches coalesce:

> Part of the talking cure is in the innumerable precise and discrete emphases of the telling that "put" or "bring" the latent contents into discourse. The effect of this transportation gives new body to the analysand's speech, as it assists the patient in bringing the force of instincts into words adequate to bear and transform them, as well as bringing the force of the instinct into that poetics of telling that is in itself a derivative of sexual life.

Question: Does the relational perspective fit into a pluralistic approach?

Answer: Yes, as long as it is not the "radical" relational view that defines mind as existing *only* in relations to others, and thus is never autonomous. Mitchell and Aron (1999, pp. xiv–xv) have stated, for example, that "Relational analysts in speaking of a 'two-person psychology' never intended to deny that there are two distinct individuals with their minds, their own histories, and their own inner worlds, which come together in the analytic situation."

Question: Did Freud recognize or anticipate a pluralistic approach?

Answer: In this connection, Jacobs (2001, p. 758) comments that Freud observed long ago that in analysis the unconscious of the patient and analyst are in continual communication. It took many years before clinicians began to make use of that insight and to explore the role that such communication plays in the analytic situation. We are just beginning to do so, and the exploration so far has proven fruitful, not only in helping us to use ourselves more effectively and creatively but to accomplish the traditional aims of psychoanalysis. Jacobs (2001, pp. 756–757) also notes perceptively that as yet we know relatively little about the meanings that are created as well as uncovered in therapy— how they affect the patient's fantasies, defenses and transferences, and how these affect the meanings that are generated. This is still a relatively unexplored aspect of the therapeutic process.

Question: What is a clinical example of Mitchell's (1988) view that "Interpretations are complex relational events?"

Answer: The following vignette is reported by Meissner (2001), who is not a radical relationist but a methodologic pluralist:

CASE REPORT:

A woman in her mid-30s, a mother, developed a view of Meissner as attacking and devaluing her, harshly critical of her every shortcoming. This view of him did not coincide with her actual experiences in the therapeutic interaction, so it surfaced as a fear of criticism; that is, although he had not been critical, she assumed he must be thinking critically of her and sooner or later would attack her with the most severe criticisms. The belief persisted despite her actual experiences with him and could not be changed by his denying any such intentions, but only gradually by exploring her childhood experiences with her narcissistic and critical mother, and also by examining other contemporary experiences in which she anticipated criticisms from others that did not materialize: "If I attempted a straightforward interpretation, it was usually experienced as critical." Gradually she developed a new and more adaptive version of her psychic reality that replaced the old maladaptive one. As her fear diminished, she became able to associate more freely and to disagree with the therapist, but from time to time she would say, "I keep thinking you're going to be critical, even though I know you won't." Her behavior outside of analysis also changed gradually from her pervious fearful inhibition to an attitude of willingness to take a stand and assert herself, even when she knew others would oppose of disapprove.

In the summary and conclusions of the same essay on psychic reality, Meissner writes (2001, p. 885):

> The nature of psychic reality prohibits any direct access on the part of one subject to the psychic reality of another. For example, countertransference responses do not involve direct knowledge of the mind of the patient nor of his unconscious, but rather reflect impressions, usually but not exclusively, that allow for *inferences about the patient's psychic reality*. Such inferences have a different status than the experiences on which they are based, and are subject to all the limitations of such inferential processes. These constraints would apply to all such inferential "intersubjective" communications, including empathy, projective identification, etc. [as well as inferences from the patient's free associations, dreams, and other clinical data]. (emphasis added)

Question: What is another example of a pluralistic approach?

Answer:

CASE REPORT:

Smith (2001, pp. 801–803) reports the case of a woman in her forties who in recent sessions had been telling him that she felt he was ignoring her erotic excitement and focusing instead on a wish to be mothered. Smith suspected (silently) that she was moving defensively from one position to the other in order to avoid the conflicts associated with both. She insisted, however, that he was afraid of her sexuality. Then one day she expressed how old she felt, how old her husband seemed, and what a mess her home and life were. She asked whether the therapist thought she was awful for that. He felt (silently) that she was seeking reassurance, but just at that moment he was distracted by something beside his chair. She asked with a challenging tone what he was doing and then added, "You are simply adjusting your chair. I am so good; I don't turn around and look." The therapist commented: "Looking would be too aggressive." She disagreed, saying it was because it would startle him. Then she paused, and in a quieter tone said, "I suddenly got aroused." At that point Smith had a number of associations, some of which were: he was struck by her sexual excitement occurring when he felt momentarily distracted, he thought of her potential embarrassment about the arousal, and about a patient who told him she had had an orgasm during a session with a previous therapist. He also had other associations. In addition, he considered the possibility that she was using erotic fantasy to reach out to him because of feeling she had lost him momentarily, so he said to her, "Notice that you got aroused just after you felt you had lost me." She said, "Perhaps," in a tone that lacked conviction. Her tone realigned his thinking, leading to his responding to another aspect of her emotional state and to the history of their relationship together. Now he said, "Or perhaps your arousal started when I said that looking at me would be too aggressive." She agreed, this time with conviction, saying that she thought it was the tone of his voice that got her excited. The therapist then said, "It felt like an invitation, a joining; you *could* look at me." "Yes," she said emphatically, but then she fell silent and after a while said that she had detached from him. Smith concluded (to himself) that when he acknowledged that it was his comment that had excited her, she pulled back defensively into a more passive, detached relation to him. "Together and sequentially we thus both avoided the erotic component of the interaction between us . . . In any given moment we do not know what may become clearer over time. Regardless of one's perspective on this particular interaction, however, we can see that there is a subtle dance of engagement and disengagement being played out between analyst and patient."

REFERENCES

Aron, L. (1996). *A meeting of minds.* Hillsdale, NJ: Analytic Press.

Bollas, C. (1997). Wording and telling sexuality. *International Journal of Psychoanalysis, 78,* 363–367.

Busch, F. (2001). Are we losing our mind? *Journal of the American Psychoanalytic Association, 49,* 739–779.

Hoffman, I. (1998). *Ritual and spontaneity in the psychoanalytic process.* Hillsdale, NJ: Analytic Press.

Jacobs, T. (2001). Commentary on, Are we losing our mind? By F. Busch. *Journal of the American Psychoanalytic Association, 49,* 752–758.

Meissner, W. (2001). Psychic reality in the psychoanalytic process. *Journal of the American Psychoanalytic Association, 49,* 855–890.

Mitchell, S. (1988). *Relational concepts in psychoanalysis.* Cambridge, MA: Harvard University Press.

Mitchell, S., & Aron, L. (Eds.). (1999). *Relational psychoanalysis.* Hillsdale, NJ: Analytic Press.

Smith, H. (2001). Hearing voices: The fate of the analyst's identifications. *Journal of the American Psychoanalytic Association, 49,* 782–812.

Index

213

About the Author

Philip F. D. Rubovits-Seitz, M.D., is Clinical Professor of Psychiatry and the Behavior Sciences at the George Washington University Medical Center in Washington, D.C. He is a Life Fellow of the American Psychiatric Association, and Member of the Washington, American, and International Psychoanalytic Associations. He was formerly a staff member of the Chicago Psychoanalytic Institute, Visiting Professor of Psychiatry at the University of Cincinnati College of Medicine, and Director of Psychiatric Research at the Indiana University Medical Center. Dr. Rubovits-Seitz has been a pioneer in investigation of the interpretive process in psychoanalysis and dynamic psychotherapy, and has published extensively in this and other subjects. He is the author of *Depth-Psychological Understanding: The Methodologic Grounding of Clinical Interpretations* (1998), *Kohut's Freudian Vision* (1999), and *The Interpretive Process: Progressive Communication of Latent Meanings* (2001). Dr. Rubovits-Seitz received the Hofheimer Award for Psychiatric Research from the American Psychiatric Association in 1955, the Annual Research Award of the Washington Psychoanalytic Society (1985), The Clinical Faculty Psychiatric Teaching Award of the George Washington University Medical Center (1985), and the Best Paper Award for 1992 from the *Journal of the American Psychoanalytic Association*.